Succeed at I.Q. Tests

Gilles Azzopardi

foulsham
LONDON • NEW YORK • TORONTO • SYDNEY

foulsham

Bennett's Close, Cippenham, Berkshire SL1 5AP

ISBN 0-572-01948-3

This English language edition copyright © 1994
W. Foulsham & Co. Ltd.
Originally published by
Marabout, Alleur, Belgium © Marabout.

Phototypeset in Great Britain by Typesetting Solutions, Slough, Berkshire.
Printed in Great Britain by Cox & Wyman Ltd, Reading, Berkshire.

CONTENTS

'All is quiet; only my heart breaks the silence.
The voice of the universe is my intelligence'.

Lamartine
(Poetic Meditations XIII, Le Lac)

INTRODUCTION

The term 'mental test' was first proposed in 1890 by the American psychologist Mick Cattell* to denote a series of psychological tests that assessed the differences between students.

In 1905 the French psychologist Alfred Binet published the first practical intelligence tests.

And in 1917 the United States brought about the use of tests to recruit army officers. This extensive use contributed to the immense popularity of the tests in Anglo-Saxon countries where, even today, they are used much more than in Europe. In Europe, the tests have always been used exclusively in civilian contexts, particularly in France, Belgium and Switzerland. Nowadays, the tests are used on a fairly everyday basis, but are essentially limited to use in schools, professional selection or indeed medical and social psychology.

*Not to be confused with R. B. Cattell who is spoken of in Chapter 2.

The Intelligence Tests

The following chart shows where intelligence tests stand in relation to other mental tests.

Intelligence tests form a part of efficiency tests which study the different understanding capacities of the personality; aptitude, understanding (cultural acquisition) and intelligence.

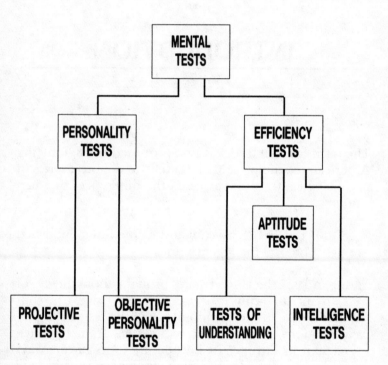

The Tests in Question

Intelligence tests have often been criticised, and still are, especially in Eastern Europe, for several reasons of which these two are the most common:

- because they support the principle of each individual being different. Men would therefore be of unequal intelligence.

- because intelligence measured by tests would only be the intelligence precisely defined by the tests. As Binet famously once quoted, 'intelligence is what my test measures'.

It is true that, as it stands today, it is still very difficult to distinguish between heredity and environment, to know whether the differences recorded are dependant on biology or cultural influences.

It is true that intelligence tests ignore certain aspects of intellectual functioning; under-estimating for example the importance of psychological and social factors.

But the tests nevertheless remain the most reliable tool in modern psychology and a very objective implement in personal appreciation.

All the tests presented in this book have been devised from models of their type so that you yourself can assess your intelligence in its general and specialised forms.

THE FORMS
OF INTELLIGENCE

Defining Intelligence

The dictionary defines intelligence under various headings, which is useful in showing its diversity. It is interesting because it shows both the extent of the notion of intelligence and its evolution.

1. The ability to know, to understand . . .

2. (In a strict sense) The unity of mental functions concerning conceptual and rational understanding (as opposed to sensation and intuition.)

3. Didactically. The ability of a human being to adapt to new situations.

4. The quality of a mind that understands and adapts easily.

These definitions correspond to two major explanations of intelligence, the dates of which are significant.

The first concept (1160), which combines intelligence with understanding, was written in a metaphysical context.

The second (1636), which links intelligence with the ability to adapt, was written in a more 'scientific' context.

Intelligence and Understanding

Since antiquity, intelligence has been regarded as an essential faculty of man, a capacity to manipulate abstract ideas. Handling abstractions, ideas and concepts, intelligence naturally contrasted with factual knowledge and concrete experience. However, when its functioning was based on sensory knowledge it proceeded in the same fashion as does the material world. Intelligence seemed to have come directly from objects of thought which, like objects of the physical world had the particularity of having been given to us, of 'pre-existing'.

From Plato to Aristotle, all the major theories of the era insist on the 'ideal' aspect of intelligence whilst neglecting the fact that what it really comes down to is technical achievements.

Intelligence and Divinity

This notion evolved with the domination of Christianity at the time of the end of the Roman empire. Intelligence was not merely a rational and natural attribute. Under the influence of the theologies at the time, it came to be considered more and more — particularly in the Middle Ages — as divine intervention in man.

Intelligence was no longer a faculty, but of divine origin, which makes all the difference in allowing us to distinguish between man and animals, to break away from nature and come closer to God, to whom we are indebted for his 'creative powers'.

Thus the notion of intelligence is very ambiguous. It belongs to the realm of consciousness, but also falls into the realm of action. More or less ignored in antiquity, the works on intelligence have been recognised by the Church even if only for the divine manifestations which can be found in them.

Intelligence and Techniques

Leading scientists have always maintained two ideas with regard to the impetus provided by techniques, which were a long time in becoming prevalent.

The first is that intelligence is not merely a capacity to seize from objects already there: it creates its own objects. It was only with, and after, Kant, that it was admitted that understanding does not come from fruits that we pick, but rather is something we grow ourselves.

The second view is that we have a practical intelligence simply because we are animals. But we must wait for the full development of industrial mechanisation, and a wide spread along evolutionary lines, in order for the use of instruments and the fabrication of tools to become criteria of intelligence.

Intelligence and Action

In the 19th century, the achievements of the industrial revolution and the success of the laws of natural selection combined to impose on people's minds the idea that knowledge must give way to action, that the time to understand must definitely take second place after the time to act.

And when in 1807 Bergson proposed replacing the term 'homo sapiens', which characterised the human being, with 'homo faber', this signified the end of one idea on intelligence. For some time, the question of intelligence was no longer really being posed by philosophers or theologians. Moving away from the speculative field, intelligence was being considered more and more as an object of observation and experimentation. It now belong to the psychological domain.

Intelligence and Adaptation

At the very beginning of the 20th century, the re-definition of intelligence fitted in with the theories on evolution. If the laws of natural selection give each species its own intelligence, then the intelligence given to man, the dominant species, must directly correspond to a superior form of adaptation.

It becomes therefore, like nutrition and reproduction, a vital function. For Binet 'it exists only because it serves a purpose ... to help us adapt better to the physical environment of nature and ... to the morals of our fellow men'.

Intelligence and Instinct

Explaining intelligence by bringing it back to knowledge or by tying it in with adaptation tends to make one come back to the same thing. To make intelligence a vital function having already made it a natural ability means once again not taking into account the massive complexities of intelligence.

Intelligence does not come down to a simple adaptation to a pre-existing reality any more than it could come down to the understanding of given objects.

Capable of creating its own objects, human intelligence stands out precisely because it invents realities other than those given by nature.

All man's achievements, aesthetic, technical or cultural are there to bear witness that intelligence is more than just a complex form of instinct; it is a genuine capacity for innovation.

Intelligence and Performance

Intelligence cannot therefore come down to adaptation unless it is limited to a technical plan. Whichever way one characterises it — from Piaget to Oleron, the formula has some success — like the adaptation of the means to the achievement of the goal.

This definition has its advantages in not being false, even if it is partial, and in being applicable, 'realistic'.

It also, importantly, allows intelligence to be observed, to be judged, or even measured according to its results and achievements.

Intelligence and Instruments

The use of instruments is not just confined to man. Animal behaviour demonstrates numerous cases of complex constructions and artefacts. For example, in their habitats (nests, burrows, etc.) and when hunting (traps . . .). Certain species, ants, beavers, bees, are even renowned for their industrious character.

But most of these activities generally come down to instinct; their behaviour is repetitive. Human activity on the other hand is more innovative. Intelligence is characterised less by the fact it makes tools than by the fact that it is constantly dreaming up 'new' instruments which are constantly becoming more and more complex.

Intelligence and Innovation

Today, at the end of the 20th Century, intelligence seems to define itself more and more as a capacity for innovation.

The present day 'tools', the mathematical, logical and linguistic systems, are unrecognisable when compared with the first prehistoric tools . . . Modern machines — computers, robots, etc. attain higher and higher levels of performance.

With the progress of computer science and artificial intelligence, intelligence is moreover seen less from the point of view of its psychological characteristics as from that of its working and operational structures.

Intellectual Functioning

What we know about intellectual functioning amounts to very little. The research biologists, neurologists, psychologists, etc. continue to put forward more hypotheses with regard to intelligence than they have certainties.

What is sure, however, is that the brain is the organ that controls intelligence.

Intelligence and the Brain

Intellectual functioning is totally dependent on the functioning of the brain. For example, we are able to observe the complete lack of intellectual activity in the case of babies born without a brain. Furthermore, we have all noticed the disappearance of these activities during sleep.

But up till now all the research to localise intelligence in the brain has come to nothing. Certain operations which condition intellectual functioning have, however, been linked to precise cerebral areas. Movement, visual perception, hearing and language all seem directly linked to certain parts of the brain. If one of these parts is damaged, physically or chemically, the corresponding operation is disrupted.

Most specialists are in agreement that the brain as a whole participates in intelligence even if, paradoxically, all of the brain is not needed for intellectual functioning. There have been cases where intelligence has scarcely been disrupted despite the removal of important parts of the brain.

Intelligence and Computers

The basic characteristics of intellectual functioning are often compared to those of a computer.

Human intelligence and the computer machine operate in a similar way by using simple or elaborate symbols (images, concepts, patterns).

They both use linking systems according to the rules of logic, arithmetic for calculation and semantics for language.

They are both capable of carrying out complex tasks by performing an elementary sequence of operations with great speed.

Finally, being very versatile they can accomplish various tasks by adapting different methods according to different objectives.

The computer is, however, far from exhausting all the resources of human intelligence. At the moment it is incapable of learning to learn and exposes its 'stupidity' when it comes to matters of judgement. This is particularly evident when faced with the problems of understanding language (translation) and complex strategy (a game of chess).

But the similarities between human intelligence and artificial intelligence are such that many people wonder whether, in the very distant future, the second won't equal the first.

In any case, this notion is sufficiently widespread to allow for intellectual functioning to be compared to a method of data processing. This is one of the two major present-day theories.

The other, a little older, considers, and even sometimes defines intelligence as a resolving of problems.

Intelligence as Problem Resolving

The Gestaltistes, who put forward this problem resolving definition of intelligence, stem from a psycho-philosophical movement which values the one above the many parts, the whole above the constituents and the unity above its elements. It is an approach which favours the global approach, immediate perceptions and intuitive solutions.

From this point of view, all situations where someone has something to understand, to do or to communicate amount simply to a more or less complex series of problems to resolve.

Moreover, there is not a great difference between a problem and its solution; it is the same situation seen from a different angle. Intelligence is there to turn a perception-problem into a perception-solution.

This type of concept has advantages in setting down the problems, limiting their difficulty and making one aware of what the difficulties really are. On the other hand, it doesn't give a lot of indication into the method of solving the problems.

Intelligence as Data Processing

The information processing theory tries less to describe intelligence as a function of observable behaviour than it does to seek internal mechanisms on the basis of which to propose certain patterns.

All the most essential intellectual activities, perception, memory and language, are considered, like the most elaborate ones, understanding and reasoning, as manipulation of the facts. There is always information to process, whether it be sorting, stocking or sending on. Thus, all the intellectual operations can be modelled and simulated by computer programmes for testing.

The advantage of this type of theory is that it allows a good description of the problems and of the procedures to enter into in order to reach a solution.

However, it is of little use in situations where it is the lack of information that creates the problem.

Yet, the distinctive feature of intelligence is also its ability to take uncertainties into account and to make evaluations and predictions on the basis of hypotheses and probabilities, etc.

Two Types of Intelligence

It is customary to single out two major types of intelligence. They have been described, and sometimes opposed to each other by various writers in fairly similar terms. Intelligence has been said to be concrete and/or abstract, practical and/or theoretical, empirical and/or logical, technical and/or formal, sensory-motor and/or rational.

What is interesting about this split is that it brings to the fore two essential concepts needed to understand intelligence; that of detour and that of model.

Intelligence and the Detour

We have all experienced the time when, to go from one point to another, the quickest route is often the longest one. The detour concept rests on this principle. Whether it be avoiding an obstacle, taking time to make a tool, or waiting for a more favourable moment it is often necessary to make a detour from an objective in order to reach it.

Intelligence always assumes a capacity for restraint, but this is not immediate. A young child shows an inability to control its impulse, to make a detour from its goal. Controlling one's impulse is firstly to do with individual development, and then with education.

Intelligence and the Model

As well as a capacity for restraint, intelligence also assumes a capacity for representation.

Unlike animals, man is capable of distancing himself

from reality. He constructs models which allow him to understand and act more efficiently when it comes to reality.

These models may be concrete (diagrams, maps, etc.) or abstract (systems, theories, etc.).

If, for example, one takes the resolving of problems, it is the notion of structure that serves as the model. In the case of treating information on the other hand, it is that of a programme. The first is more static, the second more dynamic, but whatever the case, it is a question of defining the rules of organisation and/or procedures sufficiently, in order to apply oneself to different problems. Thus the knowledge acquired while resolving one problem can be used while solving others.

But a model is not only essential to the transfer of understandings and abilities. It is also a simulation of reality, thanks to which one can 'try out' solutions in safe conditions, where errors are not punished.

INTELLIGENCE FACTORS

There are two questions to be asked here, and the different responses that can be given need careful consideration.

The first question concerns the very nature of intelligence. What is it made up of? Is it a unique faculty that has different applications, or several individual faculties which combine to make a single entity?

The second question ties in with the evaluation of intelligence. Can intellectual functioning be fully or partly measured?

The different answers to these questions will help shed light on certain aspects of intelligence.

Factorial Analysis

At the end of the last century, intelligence became an object of observation and experimentation. But very soon there turned out to be too many variables for an experiment in intellectual functioning to be really conclusive.

In 1904 an English psychologist, Charles Spearman, invented factorial analysis in order to reduce this large number of variables by bringing them down to just a few factors. Let us say, to simplify things, that factorial analysis is a mathematical method that defines the correlations between the different tests to which intelligence can be subjected.

When in use, factorial analysis reveals three types of factor:

— a general factor that one finds in all tests;

— group factors, each one particular to a certain number of tests;

— specific factors, each one particular to one test.

In fact, one only takes the first two types of factors into account. The last one is too specific to be of any relevance.

At the moment there are two concepts of factorial analysis. One comes from the English School to which Spearman and Vernon belong. The other is that of the American School (Thurstone, Guilford).

English authors have a hierarchical conception which favours a general type of intelligence (factor g). For them, each intellectual test always results in a combination of two factors (bifactorial method): a general order factor and a group factor.

On the other hand, Americans defend a multi-factorial conception where the general factor is considered as no more and no less than a group factor.

Spearman's Factor

The g factor has often been linked to intelligence. First of all, Spearman defined it as a type of mental energy produced by the brain, then as a second degree abstraction, a sort of 'conscience of the conscience'.

Nowadays, the g factor is considered more as a constant of intelligence rather than being linked to it. But its importance is not equally recognised by all. For some factorial analysis specialists it is of cardinal importance; for others, it does not exist.

In practice, however, everyone admits that there is a form of general intelligence that can keep a check on itself and measure itself using two methods.

The first method involves using a large number of very varied tests. It is this method* that is often used to measure one's intelligence quotient (I.Q.).

The other uses one unique non-verbal test**. The one used most often is the 'Progressive Matrices' test of 1938, devised by Raven and Penrose, which involves completing a sequence of drawings.

Anstey's 'dominos test', which presents a sequence of dominos to be completed, is equally much used.

The Five General Intelligence Factors of Meili

Since the beginning of the century, Spearman's g factor has been diversely interpreted. It often breaks into different factors.

Alfred Binet, who had managed the first French laboratory of experimental psychology since 1897, had already defined intelligence by its four functions: comprehension, invention, reasoning and criticism.

*This was used by the U.S. Army during the Second World War.
**The British Army used this as a test of intelligence during the last war.

During this time, Richard Meili, a Swiss psychologist was, for his part, defining five 'general intelligence factors'.

— The 'complexity' factor that would be the result of an 'intellectual tension' and would show itself by a certain number of possible calculations.

— The 'plasticity' factor corresponding to an ability to call into question established models and to learn new models.

— The 'globalisation' factor (perception and organisation of given sets).

— The 'fluidity' factor, to which intuition, creativity and intellectual innovation can be linked.

— The 'definite' factor, corresponding to diverse forms of intelligence, concrete and abstract, verbal, numerical, visual, etc.

The Seven 'Fundamental Intelligence Factors' of Thurstone

Having done a re-analysis of all the intelligence tests used before the war, Thurstone could find no trace of Spearman's general factor, but concluded that seven principal factors existed.

— A 'spatial' factor (perception and comparison of two and three-dimensional spatial figures).

— A 'perception' factor (identification of a given configuration in a complex configuration).

— A 'memory' factor (memorisation and reminiscence of sets not logically related to each other).

— A 'numerical' factor (manipulation of numbers).

— A 'verbal' factor (language comprehension).

— A 'lexical' factor (vocabulary mobilisation).

— A 'reasoning' factor (induction and deduction).

These factors, some of which (verbal and spatial) have already been isolated by Spearman as group factors, are nowadays recognised by most specialists. Almost everyone is in agreement.

These are the ones we have used in the following chapters to test your different faculties.

Guilford's Parallelepipede

In the United States in the '70s, Guilford presented the results from 20 years of experimentation in all areas of intelligence. At the end of these works, he concluded that 120 factors probably existed, by estimating that about 100 had already been isolated individually. He organised them in a spatial format.

By structuring intelligence as a three-dimensional space, Guilford put forward a classification of the different factors by systematically tying them in to three plans.

— The plan of 'operations' (basic intellectual functions) which consists of five types of activity; judgement, divergent production (creativity), convergent production (treatment of given things), memory and cognition (understanding).

— The plan of 'products' (the forms into which information is arranged) which consists of six methods of organisation: units, classes, relations, systems, transformations and implications.

— The plan of 'contents' (the types of given things) which involves four information categories: figurative, symbolic, semantic and behavioural.

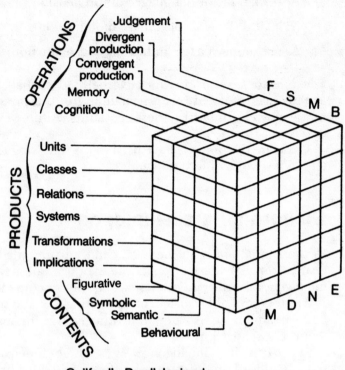

Guilford's Parallelepipede
(J. P. Guilford, *The Nature of Human Intelligence*,
New York, McGraw-Hill, 1967)

Each faculty of intelligence can therefore be described as an operation performed on one product of a particular content.

Vernon's Hierarchical System

Representing the English School, Vernon proposed a more simple and more hierarchical classification. Breaking away from the principle that one would not know how to limit the particular aptitudes, he recognised that we are gradually discovering more and more factors as more tests are carried out and more people tested.

Consequently, it seemed to him that real intelligence can be better evaluated and described with just a few factors, rather than a great many.

This is what Vernon himself presented (P. E. Vernon, *Intelligence and Cultural Environment,* London, Methuen, 1969), as the hierarchical system of aptitudes:

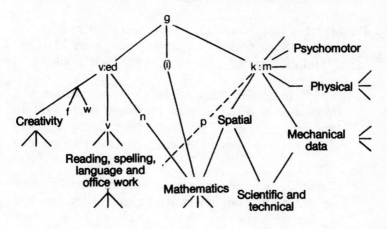

On the top level we see Spearman's general (g) factor. Then on the second level, two group factors: (v:ed) for Verbal-educational and (k:m) for Spatial mechanical; underneath we see more precise factors, some of which had been isolated by Thurstone: W for the lexical factor, V for the verbal factor, N for the numerical factor, P for the perceptive factor and F for fluidity. At the bottom we see specialised aptitudes.

Cattell's Conception

Cattell's proposal dissociates itself from those of his contemporaries by the way he differentiates so clearly between competence and performance.

This notion was first proposed by Hebb, who made a distinction between two forms of intelligence:

— Form A, corresponding to the potential intelligence of a person's inner character, probably linked to heredity.

— Form B, corresponding to an effective performance level, an intellectual output.

Cattell takes up this distinction in a certain manner by breaking up Spearman's g factor into two general factors: gf, or fluid intelligence, and gc, or cyrstallised intelligence.

— 'Fluid' intelligence is independent of surrounding influences. It is more easily measured using 'culture free' tests. These are similar to 'Progressive Matrices 1938' of Penrose and Raven, or Anstey's dominos tests.

— 'Crystallised' intelligence is, on the other hand, dependent on cultural influences; it is linked to education and experience. The tests that measure it are more specialised (verbal, numerical, memory) and more adapted to evaluate and predict scholastic success.

CALCULATE YOUR I.Q.

As we have seen, there are several ways of measuring intelligence. The notion of I.Q. is, in itself, interpreted in various ways. In its original form, which has now become obsolete, one's intellectual quotient represented a link between mental age and chronological age. This could not be applied with any validity to adults.

Nowadays, we often put systems of evaluating intelligence under the heading of intelligence quotient. In general, scores are converted into 'standard' marks which are then transformed into an I.Q. with the help of different tables, according to the age of the subject tested.

The method I propose to calculate your I.Q. is similar. It allows you to make an overall evaluation of your intellectual level. But this evaluation, helpful though it may be, is still approximate. A more precise evaluation involves the administration of more thorough exercises which involve 'performance' tests. For obvious reasons, these cannot be included in a book.

The I.Q. that you will obtain will thus be of more indicative value than absolute. The table used to transform your score into an I.Q. applies to all age groups. Consequently, it is up to you to evaluate your results. An I.Q. of 125 does not, naturally, have the same value or significance at 18 years old as at 40.

Instructions

The evaluation before you is composed of four tests, all similar in principle. They are preceded by examples, to familiarise you with the problems. Each test contains 20 questions that should be answered whilst at the same time rigidly obeying the following instructions:

— Each test lasts precisely 15 minutes.

— When these 15 minutes have passed, you may no longer correct your answers, even if you notice an error.

— You may not use any instrumental aids or ask help from anyone (the pen and paper you use should serve only to write down your answers).

— You may, if you wish, rest for two or three minutes between each test.

Some Advice

— You need just over an hour to take each test. If you wish to do it in good conditions you need more. Wait, therefore, until you are well at ease, and have a clear head before taking some of your spare time. Choose a quiet area where you will not be disturbed. Take a pen and paper and settle down comfortably.

— You have 15 minutes to answer 20 questions; on average less than a minute per question. Therefore you have no time to lose.

— Never get stuck on a question. Move onto the next one if you start to dry up! Avoid, at all times, jumping from question to question; answer the questions in order. Do not give up on one question too quickly hoping that the following ones will be 'easier'.

— Force yourself into answering the maximum number of questions as quickly as possible. It is extremely difficult, if not impossible, to give precise answers to all questions in the time given. Do not worry if, at the end of the given time, you have not provided all the answers.

— Get an alarm clock or stop-watch to prevent yourself from worrying about the time.

— Do not use a break between tests as an opportunity to check your answers. You will only doubt whether they are correct and these doubts would be detrimental to the next test.

— Do not guess your answers. You will not calculate your I.Q. on luck.

— It goes without saying, but it is perhaps better to mention: don't cheat. Do not jump pages or stages; wait until you have answered 80 questions before looking at the solutions.

Example Problems

The examples have been devised to familiarise you with the various problems posed by the following test.

Take time to study them. Think about each exercise, find the solutions and compare them with the ones we give you. Make sure you have understood the questions well, the logic in your answers and the reasons for your mistakes. Your following performance depends on them.

1. Find the missing number.

1   4   9   16   27   .

2. Find the missing letter.

A   D   I   P   .

3. Find a word which forms two different words with the letters outside the brackets.

T(. . .)LINE

4. Which is the odd word out?

Lion Tiger Cat Hyena Panther

5. Which of these is not a tree?

EMIL
CHEBE
ACLAN
YEHRCR

6. Which figure, of the five shown, completes the sequence?

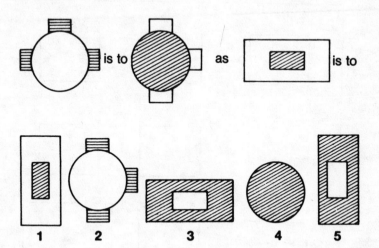

7. Which figure, out of the six shown, completes the sequence?

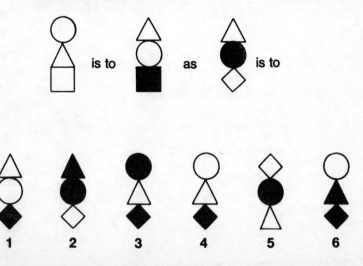

8. What figure completes the sequence?

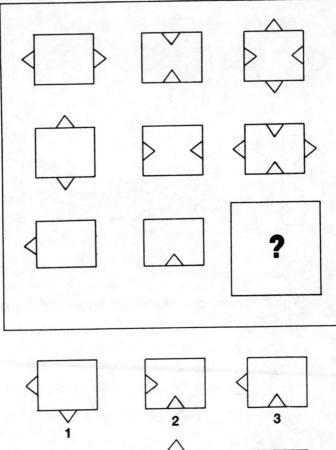

9. Which figure completes the sequence?

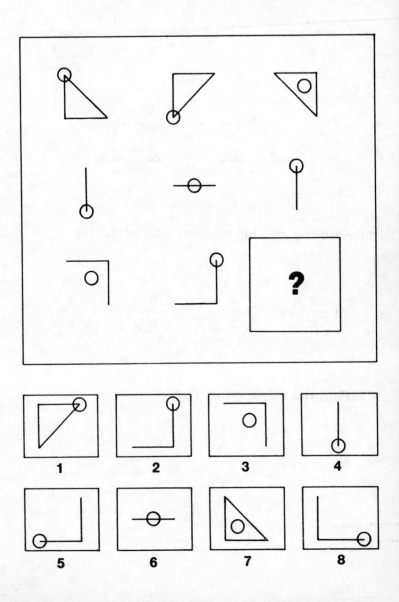

10. Which figure is the odd one out?

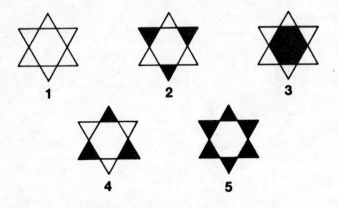

11. Find the missing number and letter.

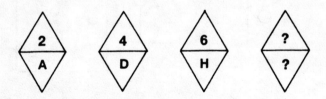

12. Find the missing number.

4	16	11
2	8	3
5	20	—

Example: solutions

PROBLEM No.	SOLUTION	EXPLANATION
1	40	It is a progression where each term follows the preceding one by the addition of consecutive prime numbers from 3 onwards. 1 (+3=) 4 (+5=) 9 (+7=) 16 (+11=) 27 (+13=) 40.
2	Y	A D I P . : It is an alphabetical sequence where each letter is separated from the preceding one by 2, 4, 6, 8 other letters. A (bc) D (efgh) I (jklmno) P (qrstuvwx) Y.
3	HEM	
4	HYENA	All the others belong to the cat family.
5	ACLAN	An anagram of canal. The others are anagrams of lime, beech and cherry.
6	5	The rectangle, like the circle, turns a quarter of a turn and the colours of its surfaces (white and grey) are reversed.
7	3	The top shapes change places. The bottom shape stays in the same position but changes colour.
8	6	On each line, the right hand figure has triangles on all sides where they occur in the previous two figures, inversing interior/exterior.

PROBLEM No.	SOLUTION	EXPLANATION
9	8	On all three lines, the figure pivots a quarter of a turn each time while the circle systematically occupies a different position; top, bottom or centre.
10	1	Figures 2 + 4, as well as 3 + 5, make pairs by inverting the colours.
11		The numbers add two each time: 2 (+2=) 4 (+2=) 6 (+2=) 8. The letters follow a growing alphabetical sequence. D is the third letter after a, H is the fourth after D, M is the fifth after H.
12	15	On each line, the last number on the right is obtained by multiplying the first by four and subtracting five. 4 (×4=) 16 (−5=) 11 2 (×4=) 8 (−5=) 3 5 (×4=) 20 (−5=) 15

STOP: THIS IS WHERE THE REAL TEST BEGINS. HAVE YOU READ THE PRECEDING INSTRUCTIONS CAREFULLY?

If you have understood, you can begin. If not, go back to the beginning of the chapter.

Fetch a pen and paper to take down your answers. You will save time checking them. Remember that you must strictly obey the time limits given for each test.

Test I

1. **Find the missing number.**

   1   4   7   10   .

2. **Find the missing numbers.**

   7   9   8   10   9   .   .

3. **Underline the anagram that is not a famous author.**

   DEWLI
   EVOKHCH
   SHOLT
   WINAT

4. **Find a word which, when placed in brackets, forms two different words with the letters outside the brackets.**

   Y(...)RING

5. **Which figure is the odd one out?**

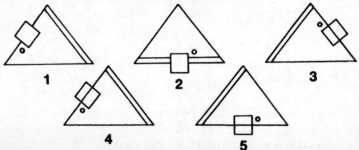

6. Which figure completes the sequence?

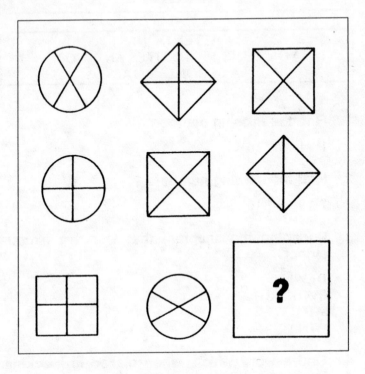

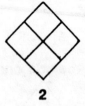

1

2

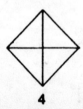

3

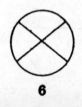

4

5

6

7. **Find the missing number.**

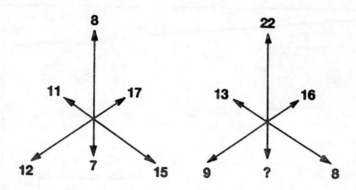

8. **Find the missing letter.**

   F I M P .

9. **Find another word to replace 'drop' between brackets.**

   F + (drop) = blossom

10. **Fill in the brackets to form two different words. (synonym:join)**

    B(. . . .)AGE

11. **Underline the word on the second line that has something in common with those on the first line.**

    ILL MAR ARK

    Arm Opt Ten Urn Fit Box

12. **Which of the following is not a European city?**

    ASRIP
    LAMNI
    HIDLE
    INEC

13. Which figure completes the sequence?

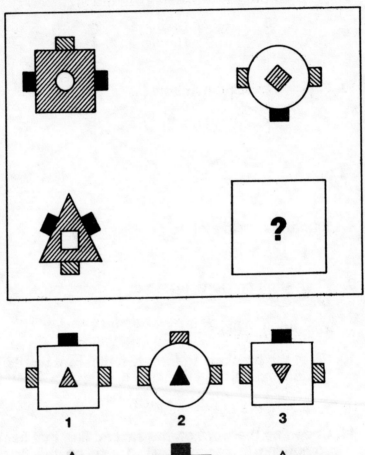

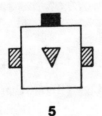 

1   2   3

4   5   6

14. Fill in the brackets on the third line with a word that has the same meaning as the first two.

> Daring
> Heroic
> (. . . .)

15. Find the missing number.

4	3	2	5
9	5	3	11
11	7	5	.

16. Find the missing number.

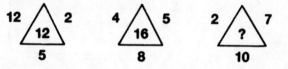

17. Fill in the brackets with a word that forms two different words with the letters outside.
(synonym:exit)

> R(. . . .)SIDE

18. Complete the sequence.

A C A E A G A K A M A

19. Fill in the brackets.

> Swathe (Hunt) Unload
> Phrase (. . . .) Against

20. Which figure goes in the square?

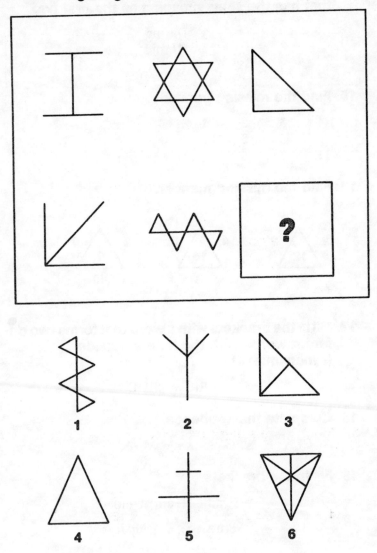

Test II

1. **Which is the odd word out.**

   Lake Ocean River Pond Puddle

2. **Which animal is the odd one out?**

   Dolphin Shark Tuna Bream Bass

3. **Fill in the brackets.**

   Incline (Lean) Not fat

   Abstain (. . . . . . .) Chorus of a song

4. **Find the missing number.**

1	6	5
7	8	1
4	7	.

5. **Find the missing numbers.**

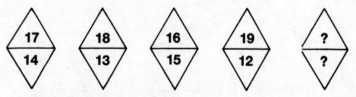

6. **Fill in the brackets with a word that forms two different words with the letters outside. (synonym:frozen water)**

   N(. . .)CAP

7. Which figure completes the sequence?

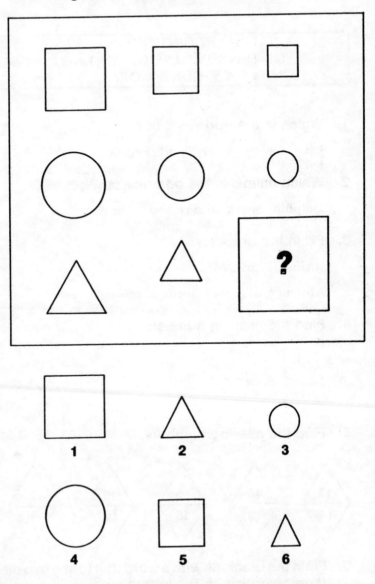

8. **Find the missing number.**

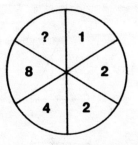

9. **Fill in the brackets with a word that forms different words with the preceding letters.**

P
PLI
SC   (...)
W
GR

10. **Which of the following anagrams is not a type of dance?**

LERE
HYSWIK
INTUME
BRAUM

11. **Fill in the brackets on the second line using the letters outside the brackets.**

ET (JUPITER) PU
TA (R..I..E) DA

12. **Find the missing letter.**

H	M	C
J	N	F
L	O	—

13. Which figure goes in the square?

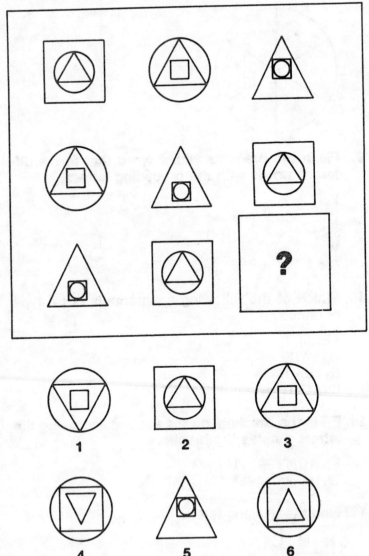

14. Which is the odd figure out?

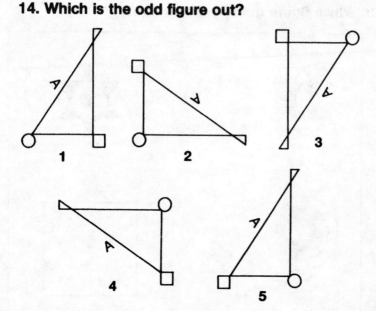

15. Which city is the odd one out?

London   Paris   Rome   Bonn

Tokyo   New York   Moscow   Canberra

16. Find the missing letters.

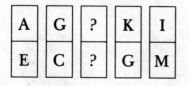

A	G	?	K	I
E	C	?	G	M

17. Find the next number in sequence.

1   2   5   12   27   .

18. Find the missing number.

4   5   6   8   .   14   18   26

19. Which figure goes in the square?

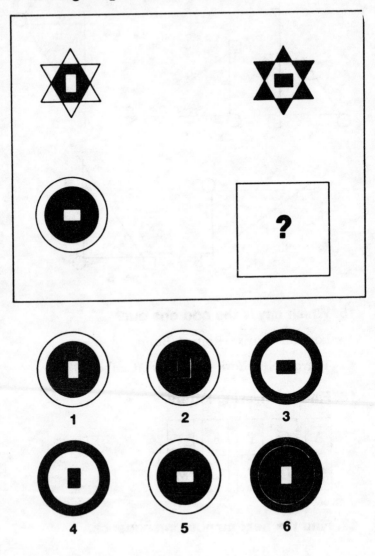

20. Which figure completes the sequence?

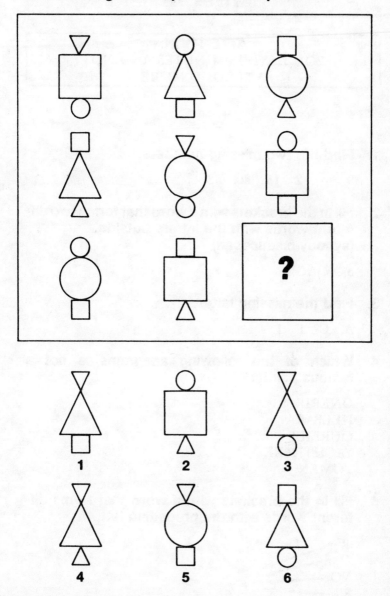

Test III

> **ATTENTION:**
> YOU HAVE 15 MINUTES AND NOT
> A SECOND MORE

1. **Find the two missing numbers.**

   3   6   12   15   30   33   .   .

2. **Fill in the brackets with a word that forms two different words with the letters outside.**
   (synonym:saucepan)

   S(. . .)AGE

3. **Find the missing letter.**

   A   C   F   J   .

4. **Which of the following anagrams is not a famous painter?**

   ONERIR
   HELPARA
   OURLILT
   YACHTRAKE
   TOMEN

5. **Fill in the brackets with a word that forms different words with the preceding letters.**

   R
   D
   VO
   SP   (. . .)
   N
   THR

6. Which figure goes in the square?

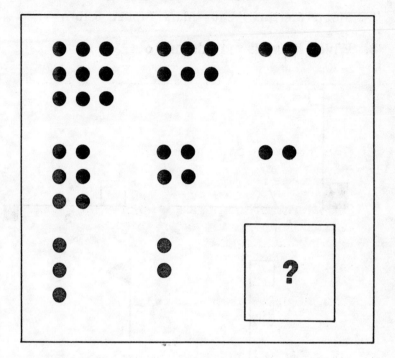

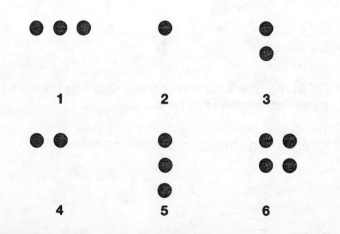

7. Which is the odd word out?

Moon Mercury Venus Mars Jupiter Saturn

8. Which figure is the odd one out?

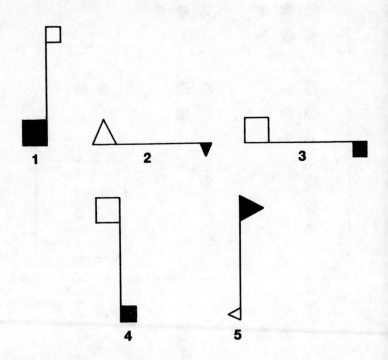

9. Fill in the brackets with a word that has the same meaning as the first two.

Opponent
Antagonist
(. . .)

10. Which figure completes the sequence?

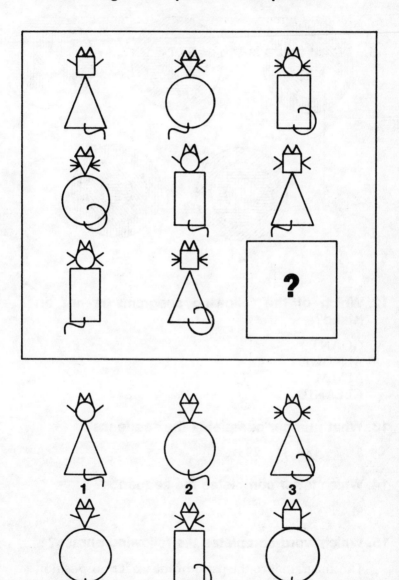

11. Which figure is the odd one out?

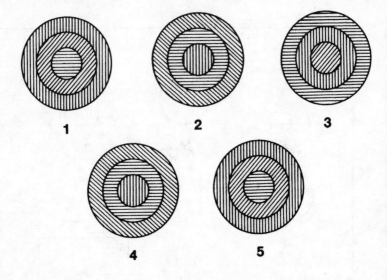

1   2   3

4   5

12. Which of the following anagrams is not an island?

GOANT
ALNDOP
ATALM
CLEANID

13. What number completes the sequence?

5   7   18   31   293   .

14. Which letter completes the sequence?

M   P   K   R   I   T   .

15. Which word completes the following phrase?

The anagram is to the palindrome what transposition is to . . .

disorder, rearrangement, synonym, reversal, identification.

16. Which word completes the phrase?

A cloud is to rain what lightning is to ...

Sky Wind Thunder Flash Sun

17. Which number completes the table?

7	21	8
17	—	5
12	1	23

18. Fill in the brackets.

EN(FORT)SU
VH(....)ME

19. Find the missing number.

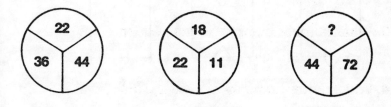

20. Which figure completes the sequence?

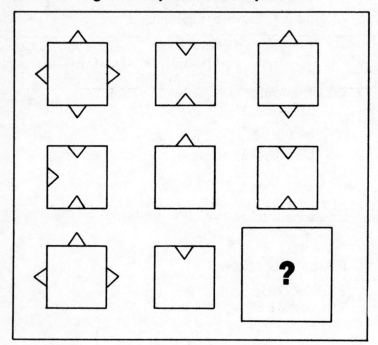

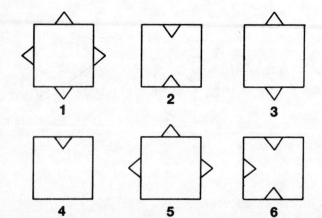

Test IV

ATTENTION:
YOU HAVE 15 MINUTES AND NOT
A SECOND MORE

1. Find the missing number.

3   9   15   21   .

2. Which number completes the table?

5	11	6
9	16	7
8	—	4

3. Which is the odd animal out.

Eagle, Owl, Bat, Tawny Owl, Eagle Owl.

4. Which is the odd word out?

Curious Absent Depart Nomad Opera.

5. Fill in the brackets with a word that forms two different words with the letters outside.

Slip(. . . . .)Lined

6. Fill in the brackets.

Final (End) Ultimate
Chalice (. . .) Beaker

7. Which figure completes the sequence?

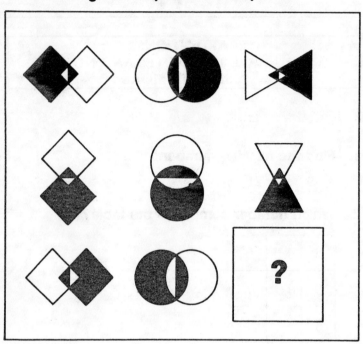

1   **2**   **3**

4   **5**   **6**

8. Find the missing number.

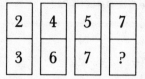

9. Find the missing number.

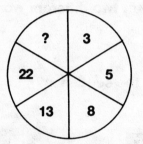

10. Find the missing number.

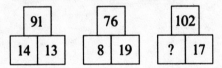

11. Fill in the brackets with a word that forms two different words with the letters outside.

GR (. . .) IOSE

12. Find the odd word out.

Deer   Golf   Race   Room

13. Find the missing letter and number.

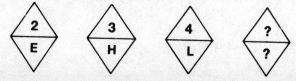

14. Fill in the brackets with a word that has the same meaning as both the words outside.

Uncommon (. . . .) Uncooked

15. Complete the second line.

Ravioli	1324564	Air	452
Viola	46785	Oil	.

16. Fill in the brackets to form two different words with the letters outside.

EA (. .) IN

17. Which figure completes the sequence?

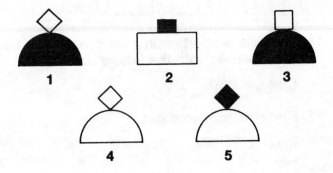

18. Find the missing letter.

E J . Z

19. Which figure completes the sequence?

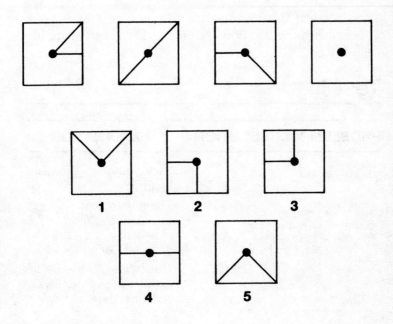

1   **2**   **3**

4   **5**

20. Fill in the brackets.

53 (face) 16
15 (....) 49

Your Score

Each correct answer is worth two points. Check your answers with the solutions given and keep your score for each test.

Test I

PROBLEM No.	SOLUTION	EXPLANATION
1	13	Each number increases by three.
2	11 10	The progression is: +2, −1: 7 (+2=) 9 (−1=) 8 (+2=) 10 (−1=) 9 (+2=) 11 (−1=) 10.
3	SHOLT	Holst was a composer. The authors are:Wilde, Twain and Checkhov.
4	EAR	
5	5	The double bar of the triangle turns clockwise and the other elements turn anti-clockwise.
6	4	On each line there are the same shapes, circle, square and diamond. The lines alternate between being diagonal and perpendicular.
7	10	The number is obtained by adding together the three exterior numbers and subtracting the two internal numbers.

PROBLEM No.	SOLUTION	EXPLANATION
		$(8 + 12 + 15) - (11 + 17)$ $= 7$ $(22 + 9 + 8) - (13 + 16)$ $= 10$
8	T	Each letter is separated by two and three letters of the alphabet alternately: F (gh) I (jkl) M (no) P (qrs) T.
9	LOWER	
10	LINK	
11	TEN	They are all three letter word beginnings of States of America: Illinois, Maryland, Arkansa, Tennesse.
12	HIDLE	Delhi is in India; the European cities are Paris, Milan, and Nice.
13	3	The circle in the square becomes a square in a circle, each of the two shapes retaining their initial colours. The double squares, however, change colour, and the single square changes position and colour.
14	BOLD	
15	13	The last number on each line is obtained by adding together the first two numbers and subtracting the third. $4 + 3 - 2 = 5$ $9 + 5 - 3 = 11$ $11 + 7 - 5 = 13$

PROBLEM No.	SOLUTION	EXPLANATION
16	14	The number is obtained by multiplying together the exterior numbers and dividing the result by 10. $12 \times 2 \times 5 = 120:10 = 12$ $4 \times 5 \times 8 = 160:10 = 16$ $2 \times 7 \times 10 = 140:10 = 14$
17	OUT	
18	Q	C is the third letter of the alphabet. The sequence of letters between the A's represent prime numbers: C (3) E (5) G (7) K (11) M (13) and Q (the 17th letter of the alphabet).
19	SAGA	The first and last letters of the word in brackets are the fifth and fourth letters of the left hand word. The second and third letters are the first two letters of the right hand word.
20	5	On each line the figures alternate between having three lines that make at least one right-angle, or six lines that make not a single one.

Test II

PROBLEM No.	SOLUTION	EXPLANATION
1	OCEAN	All the others are stretches of inland water.
2	DOLPHIN	The only mammal among fish.
3	REFRAIN	The word between the brackets is a synonym of the two words either side.
4	3	The third number on each line is obtained by subtracting the first number from the second. $6 - 1 = 5, 8 - 7 = 1,$ $7 - 4 = 3.$
5		In the top triangle the progression is: $+1, -2, +3, -4 \ldots$ In the bottom triangle the progression is: $-1, +2, -3, +4 \ldots$ $17(+1=) \ 18(-2=) \ 16(+3=)$ $19(-4=) \ 15$ $14(-1=) \ 13(+2=) \ 15(-3=)$ $12(+4=) \ 16$
6	ICE	
7	6	Each line has the same figure decreasing in size.
8	32	Each number is obtained by multiplying the preceding number by the one that follows: $1 \times 2 = 2, 2 \times 2 = 4, 2 \times 4 = 8, 4 \times 8 = 32.$
9	ANT	Which forms the words: pant, pliant, scant, want, grant.

PROBLEM No.	SOLUTION	EXPLANATION
10	HYSWIK	Whisky is a drink. The others are dances: reel, minuet and rumba.
11	RADIATE	The second and third letters of the word in brackets are the two right hand letters, reversed. The fifth and sixth letters are the two left hand letters, reversed.
12	1	Working downwards in vertical columns, the first column has breaks of one letter, the second column no letters and the third column has breaks of two letters. H (i) J (k) L MNO C (de) F (gh) I
13	3	Each figure is made up of three shapes: square, circle, triangle. On each line each of these shapes takes the interior, central and exterior position in turn.
14	5	The figure turns 90° each time, and the square and circle change places. Figure 5 does not follow the sequence.
15	NEW YORK	New York is the only city that is not a capital.
16	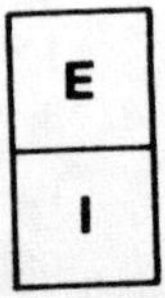 E I	The letters zig zag alphabetically from top to bottom, with a gap of one letter each time. A (b) C (d) E (f) G (h) I and E (f) G (h) I (j) K (l) M

PROBLEM No.	SOLUTION	EXPLANATION
17	58	The number 2 is multiplied to a higher power each time, and the next whole number is subtracted from the result. $1\ (=2^1-1)\ 2\ (=2^2-2)\ 5$ $(=2^3-3)\ 12\ (=2^4-4)\ 27$ $(=2^5-5)\ 58\ (=2^6-6)$
18	10	There are two number sequences: 4, 6, 10, 18 and 5, 8, 14, 26, where each number is equal to the preceding number multiplied by two, minus two. $6 = (4\times2)-2,\ 10 = (6\times2)$ $-2,\ 18 = (10\times2)-2$ $8 = (5\times2)-2,\ 14 = (8\times2)$ $-2,\ 26 = (14\times2)-2$
19	4	In the second figure of each line, the surfaces change colour and the interior rectangle turns 90°.
20	3	Each figure is made up of three shapes: square, triangle, circle. These shapes are present on each line.

Test III

PROBLEM No.	SOLUTION	EXPLANATION
1	66 and 69	The progression is: +3, ×2. 3 (+3=) 6 (×2=) 12 (+3=) 15 (×2=) 30 (+3=) 33 (×2=) 66 (+3=) 69
2	POT	
3	O	ACFJO: It is an alphabetical progression where C is the second letter after A, F is the third letter after C, J is the fourth after F, O is the fifth after J.
4	YACHTRAKE	Thackery is a writer; the painters are: Renoir, Raphael, Utrillo, and Monet.
5	ICE	Which forms the words: Rice, Dice, Voice, Spice, Nice, Thrice.
6	2	On each line the figure loses an element from one figure to the next.
7	MOON	The Moon is not a planet, but a satellite.
8	4	Figures 1 and 3, and 2 and 5 are pairs in which the segments turn 90° each time and the elements change colour.
9	FOE	
10	2	The body and head of the cats are made up of three symbols that are found on

PROBLEM No.	SOLUTION	EXPLANATION
		each line. The tail is either going to the right, the left, or rolled up. The whiskers have either two, four or six lines.
11	3	Figures 1 and 5 and 2 and 4 are identical pairs.
12	ALNDOP	Poland is a country. The islands are Tonga, Malta and Iceland.
13	668	The third number is obtained by squaring the first number and subtracting the second and so on. $5^2-7=18$, $7^2-18=31$, $18^2-31=293$, $31^2-293=668$
14	G	The solution is an alphabetical progression where each letter is separated from the following one by 2, 4, 6, 8, 10, 12 letters, alternately forwards and backwards. M (no) P (onml) K (lmnopq) R (qponmlkj) I (jklmnopqrs) T (srqponmlkjih) G.
15	REVERSAL	An anagram is a word created by changing the order of letters in another word; a palindrome is a group of words that stays the same, whether read from left to right or right to left.
16	FLASH	
17	14	On each line, the sum of all the numbers added together is 36.

PROBLEM No.	SOLUTION	EXPLANATION
18	WILD	The letters WI follow VH in the alphabet. The letters LD precede ME in the alphabet.
19	88	The numbers in the second circle are those of the first circle, divided by two. Those in the third circle are those of the first, multiplied by two.
20	3	The triangles outside the square have a positive value. The interior triangles have a negative value. The third figure is a result of the first two. $+ 4 - 2 = + 2$ $- 3 + 1 = - 2$ $+ 3 - 1 = + 2$

Test IV

PROBLEM No.	SOLUTION	EXPLANATION
1	27	Each number increases by six each time.
2	12	The middle number is obtained by adding together the two either side.
3	BAT	A bat is a mammal, all the others are birds.
4	CURIOUS	The others begin with two consecutive letters of the alphabet.
5	STREAM	
6	CUP	The word inside the brackets is a synonym of the words outside the brackets.
7	5	The figures on the bottom line are the same as those on the top line, but the colours are inverted.
8	10	The bottom numbers are obtained by multiplying the top numbers by two and subtracting $-1, -2, -3, -4$: $3 = (2 \times 2) - 1, 6 = (4 \times 2) - 2$ $7 = (5 \times 2) - 3$, $10 = (7 \times 2) - 4$.
9	39	Each number is obtained by multiplying the preceding number by two and subtracting $-1, -2, -3, -4, -5$.

PROBLEM No.	SOLUTION	EXPLANATION
		$5 = (3 \times 2) - 1$, $8 = (5 \times 2) - 2$, $13 = (8 \times 2) - 3$, $22 = (13 \times 2) - 4$, $39 = (22 \times 2) - 5$.
10	12	The bottom left number is always equal to the top number divided by the bottom right number and then by two.
11	AND	
12	RACE	The others form words when read backwards.
13	5/Q	The top number increases by one each time. This number determines the amount of letters separating the preceding letter from the one underneath. H is two letters (fg) after E, L is three letters (ijk) after H, Q is four letters (mnop) after L.
14	RARE	
15	879	The letters of the word ravioli are allocated numbers. Those numbers are allocated to the following words but with the addition of 1, then 2, then 3.
16	CH	
17	5	The second figure of each pair is cut in half. The interior shape moves outside and turns 90°. All the surfaces change colour.

PROBLEM No.	SOLUTION	EXPLANATION
18	Q	Each letter is found from its numerical position in the alphabet. The numbers are equal to the square of 2, 3, 4 and 5, plus 1. $5 \ (E) = 2^2 + 1$ $10 \ (J) = 3^2 + 1$ $17 \ (Q) = 4^2 + 1$ $26 \ (Z) = 5^2 + 1$
19	4	The only one of all the figures that does not form a right-angle.
20	IDEA	The letters of the words are numbered according to their positions in the alphabet, and these numbers are given outside the brackets. The order of the letters required is from right to left. 53 (FACE) 16 15 (IDEA) 49

What is your intelligence quotient?

You now have everything you need to work out your I.Q.

Check your correct answers once more and refer to the following table:

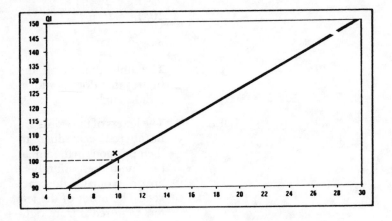

This table allows you to transform your score into an I.Q. To do that, you must:

— Add up all the correct answers you obtained in tests 1 and 2.

— Mark this total on the horizontal line of the graph (the example shows 10).

— Draw a perpendicular that passes through this point to the diagonal line on the graph. Where the lines cross, mark an X.

— Trace the horizontal from point X to the vertical on the graph. The point where this line cuts the vertical gives you an I.Q. (This example given is 100).

— Do the same with the results you obtained in tests III and IV. This will give you another I.Q.

These two values, which often vary, show you how the efficacy of intelligence can change from one moment to the next, even in the same 'working' hour.

Add these values together and divide by two to obtain your I.Q. This will give you a more realistic value. But you should only take these two values as valid if you obtained between 10 and 21 correct answers. Out of the 40 questions presented in the two tests you can, in principle, do no better or worse than that.

How you rate

- Between 90 and 110 — You have an average I.Q. You are no genius, but not a disaster either. You have no difficulty in resolving everyday problems.

- Between 110 and 120 — You are 'better than average', with an ability to solve problems quickly and efficiently with flashes of brilliance.

- Between 120 and 130 — You are either greatly on form intellectually at the moment or particularly gifted at resolving the sort of problems posed in these tests. A more complete evaluation would be preferable to confirm your performance.

- Below 90 or above 130 — (Less than 10 correct answers or more than 21 for the two tests). You fall into the categories of 'deficient' or 'greatly gifted'. The probability that you are one or the other is extremely small. It might be better to admit that this type of test is not suited to correctly evaluating your degree of intelligence.

To finish, here is a table devised by Wechsler. It allows you to place yourself intellectually in relation to the rest of the population.

I.Q.	Intellectual level	Percentage of population
130 plus	Very high	2.2%
120-129	High	6.7%
110-119	Above average	16.1%
90-109	Average	50.0%
80-89	Below average	16.1%
70-79	Low	6.7%
Less than 69	Deficient	2.2%

THE REASONING FACTOR

The reasoning factor refers to one's ability to reason in general terms; an ability to form and link together judgements in order to arrive at a conclusion.

It breaks down into two particular factors: an 'Induction' factor and a 'Deduction' factor.

Induction is a mental operation that consists of progressing from facts and particular cases to a general rule. The induction factor characterises this ability to reason from the particular to the general. For example, it is always necessary in the tests to understand the link between two elements in order to apply the rule in a third case.

Deduction is the thought process that allows a quite different application, namely to arrive at a conclusion from given rules. The deduction factor characterises the ability to reason from generalities to particulars.

These two factors are greatly in evidence in the numerous intelligence tests that exist. In reality, they are often difficult to separate. But it is universally admitted that numbers sequences are strongly associated with the D factor (deduction), and letters sequences with the I factor (induction).

The Tests

The tests are devised to help you to pinpoint your logic faculties. They conform to the models used by professional organisations or public institutions. They will allow you to evaluate your reasoning capacities and qualities as precisely as possible.

They consist of two tests, each one containing three series of exercises. This makes a total of 40 problems. Each test (20 problems) is limited in length to 15 minutes, or just under one minute per problem. Your thinking time is limited, therefore, so do not get stuck on a particular problem.

You are not obliged to take both tests at the same time. You may take your time between the two — whether you take them on the same day or not is not important.

There is, however, one condition. Wait until you have taken both tests before checking the results.

Each test is preceded by examples to familiarise you with the problems posed. Take your time to study them well.

Test I

Example: problems

1. Find the missing number.

1   4   9   16   .

2. Which numbers complete the sequence?

3   9   27   81   .   .

3. Find the missing letter.

a   e   i   o   u   .

4. Which letter completes the last group?

DBAC   HFEG   LJIK   PNM.

5. Fill in the brackets.

666(S)   389(T)   972(N)   707(.)

6. Fill in the dot.

charm   infamy   intermingle   owl
  5   6   11

Examples: solutions

1.   1 4 9 16 (25) The progression is that of whole numbers, squared.

2.   3 9 27 81 (243) (729): Each number is obtained by multiplying the previous number by three.

3. a e i o u (y): All are vowels.

4. DBAC HFEG LJIK PNM(O): In each group, the last letter precedes the first one alphabetically.

5. 666(S) 389(T) 972(N) 707(S): The letter in brackets corresponds to the first letter of the number when written down: S for Six hundred and sixty six, etc.

6.   charm   infancy   intermingle   owl
           5   6   11   (3)

The number below each word represents the number of letters in that word.

> **STOP:** THIS IS WHERE THE REAL TESTS BEGIN. HAVE YOU READ THE PRECEDING INSTRUCTIONS WELL?

Yes? Then its down to you. Don't forget that your pen and paper must be used only to write down you answers. Remember: you have 15 minutes and not a second more.

The Numbers Sequence

Each dot represents a number that you must find to complete the sequence.

1. 1 5   9   13 .
2. 5 2   4   1   3   .
3. 3 6   5   10 9   .
4. 3 6   5   15 14 . .
5. 0 2   6   12 .
6. 7 13 8   12 . 11 .

The Letters Sequence

You must replace each dot with the corresponding letter.

1. A D G J .

2. AE BF CG DH ..

3. A Z BC YX DEF ...

4. A C E G I . .

5. A D I P .

6. C G L R .

The Combined Sequence

Each dot represents a letter or number that you must find to complete the sequence.

1. J 2 G 5 D 8 . .

2. A1 BC2 DEF6 GHIJ.

3. I1   VI3   V2   XV4
    XX4   VII4   III3   XIV.

4. I2   A1   R3   AIR
    A2   M1   N3   ...

5. 1A   2D   3I   4P   ..

6. 12B   23F   34L   45.

7. A21   E72   C63   H9.

8. 111   1111   11   1; T   F   T   .

END OF THE FIRST TEST
You may either continue or wait until later.

(Solutions: Page 105-107)

Test II

Example: problems

1. **What is the hidden card?**

 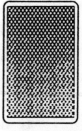

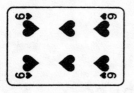 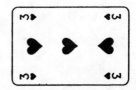

2. What are the hidden cards?

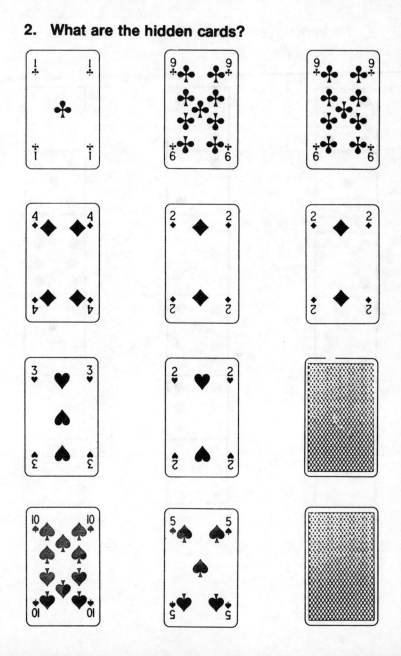

3. Fill in the missing domino.

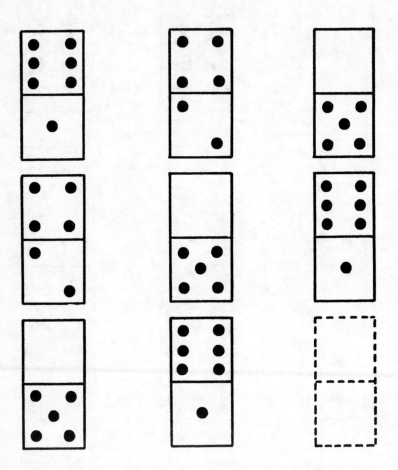

4. Fill in the missing domino.

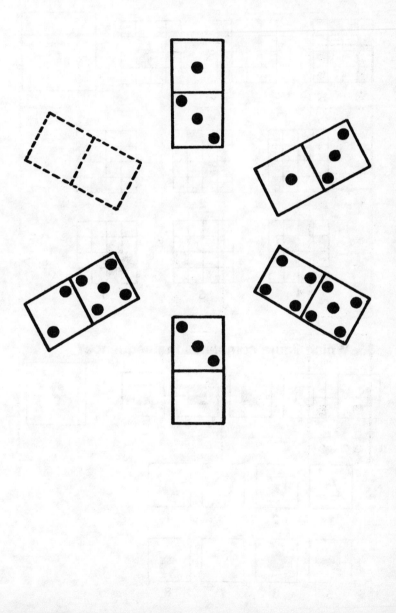

5. Which figure completes the sequence?

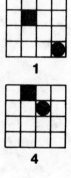 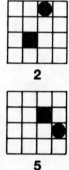

1 2 3

4 5 6

6. Which figure completes the sequence?

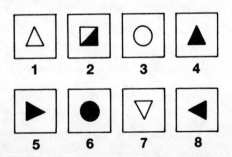

Examples: solutions

1. Seven of clubs. On each line, the cards are of the same suit, and when added together their value always equals nine.

2. Six of hearts plus two of spades. On each line, the cards are of the same suit: Clubs, diamonds, hearts and spades. In the first and third lines, the value of the right hand cards is obtained by multiplying together the two cards that precede it. In the second and fourth lines, the value of the right hand cards is found by dividing the left hand card by the middle card.

3. 4 and 2. The same sequence of dominos is present on each line, but in a different order.

4. 4 and 2. The exterior numbers of each domino progress clockwise, with a gap of one number between each. The interior numbers always amount to six when added to the domino half that is opposite.

5. 3. The square moves one place horizontally each time, the circle moves one place vertically each time.

6. 2. The shape at the centre of each square always contains a right angle.

STOP: THIS IS WHERE THE SECOND TEST BEGINS. YOU HAVE 15 MINUTES AND NOT A SECOND MORE.

The Cards Sequence

Each grey rectangle represents a hidden card that you must find. Jokers are not in the solutions.

1. What is the hidden card?

2. What is the hidden card?

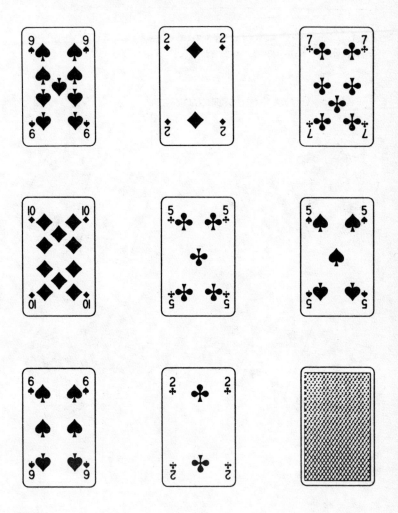

3. What are the hidden cards?

4. What is the hidden card?

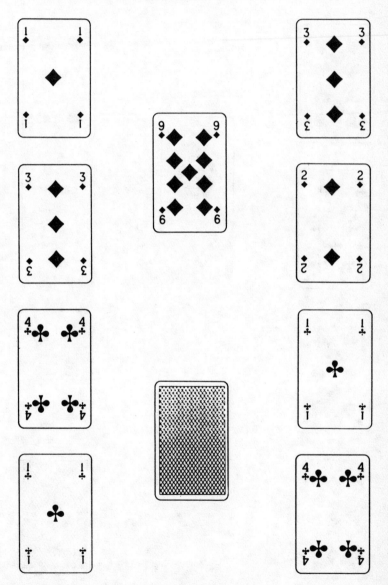

5. What is the hidden card?

6. What is the hidden card?

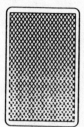

The Dominos Sequence

You must find the value of each domino shown in dashes in the picture.

1. What is the missing domino?

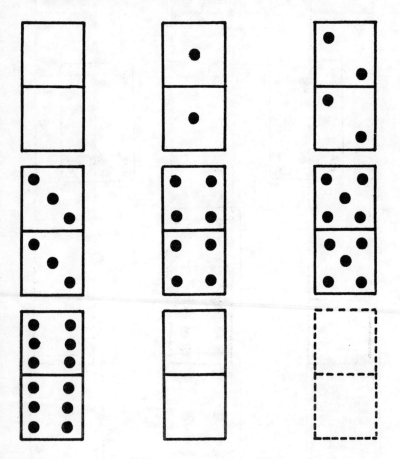

2. What is the missing domino?

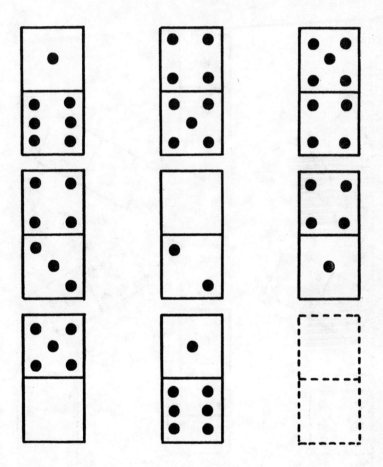

3. What is the missing domino?

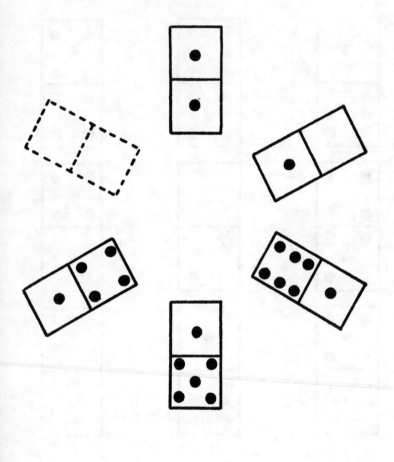

4. What is the missing domino?

5. What are the missing dominos?

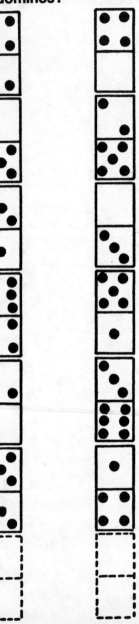

6. **What is the missing domino?**

The Graphics Sequence

Here you must complete the sequence of geometric drawings with one of the proposed figures.

1. What is the missing figure?

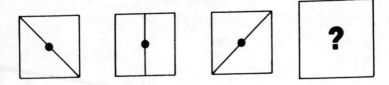

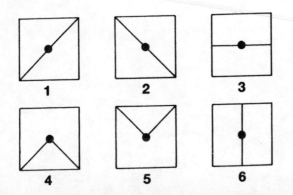

2. What is the missing figure?

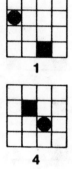 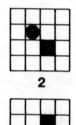

1   2   3

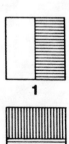

4   5   6

3. What is the missing figure?

1   2   3

4   5   6

4. What is the missing figure?

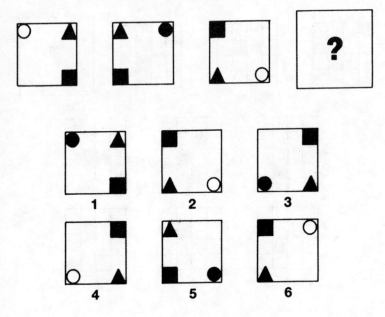

5. What is the missing figure?

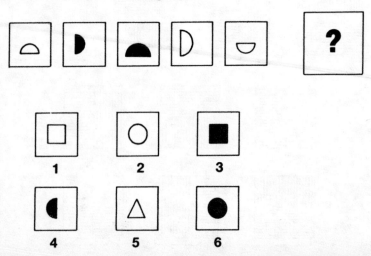

6. What is the missing figure?

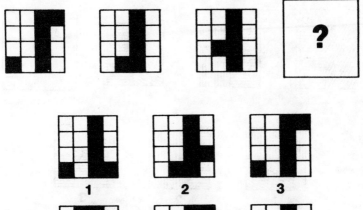

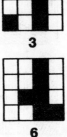

7. What is the missing figure?

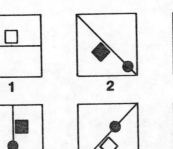

8. What is the missing figure?

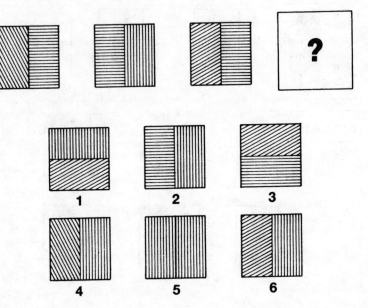

Your Score

Each correct answer is worth one point. Check your answers with the help of these solutions given and keep a list of your correct answers for each sequence.

Test I

PROBLEM No.	SOLUTION	EXPLANATION

The Numbers Sequence

1	17	Each number is obtained by adding four to the preceding one.
2	0	The progression is: -3, $+2$: $5(-3) = 2(+2) = 4(-3) = 1(+2) = 3(-3) = 0$.
3	18	The progression is: $\times 2$, -1: $3 (\times 2) = 6 (-1) = 5 (\times 2) = 10 (-1) = 9 (\times 2) = 18$.
4	56.55	The progression is: $\times 2$, -1, $\times 3$, -1, $\times 4$, -1 . . .: $3 (\times 2=) 6 (-1=) 5 (\times 3=) 15 (-1=) 14 (\times 4=) 56 (-1=) 55$.
5	20	The progression is 1, 2, 3, 4, 5 with each number squared and then subtracted by itself. $1^2 - 1 = 0, 2^2 - 2 = 2, 3^2 - 3 = 6, 4^2 - 4 = 12, 5^2 - 5 = (20)$.
6	9, 10	Each number alternately increases or decreases by an amount following the series. 6, 5, 4, 3, 2, 1: $7 (+6=) 13 (-5=) 8 (+4=) 12 (-3=) 9 (+2=) 11 (-1=) 10$.

PROBLEM No.	SOLUTION	EXPLANATION

The Letters Sequence

1	M	Each letter is separated from the preceding one by two letters: A (bc) D (ef) G (hi) J (kl) M.
2	EI	The left hand letters and the right hand letters increase alphabetically: A, B, C, D, E and E, F, G, H, I.
3	WVU	There are two alphabetical progressions; one going forwards (A, BC, DEF) the other in reverse (Z, YX, WVU), with each group increasing by one letter each time.
4	K and M	Each letter is separated by three other letters alphabetically: A (bcd) E (fgh) I (jkl) M and C (def) G (hij) K.
5	Y	The progression of the letters in this sequence is determined by their position in the alphabet. This position corresponds to a position of whole numbers, squared: $1^2 = 1 = A$, $2^2 = 4 = D$, $3^2 = 9 = I$, $4^2 = 16 = P$, $5^2 = 25 = Y$, the 25th letter of the alphabet.
6	W	Each letter in this sequence is alphabetically situated at an equal distance between two vowels: (a) b C d (e) f G h (i) j k L m n (o) p q R s t (u) v W x (y).

PROBLEM No.	SOLUTION	EXPLANATION
The Combined Sequence		
1	A and 11	Each letter, in a reversed alphabet, is separated from the preceding one by two other letters. Each number is obtained by adding three to the preceding one.
2	24	From two onwards, each number is obtained by multiplying the preceding one by the number of letters before it.
3	5	Each number (Arabic) corresponds to the number of lines that make up the Roman letter that precedes it.
4	MAN	The numbers determine the letters position in the word.
5	5Y	Each number, squared, corresponds to a letter in the alphabet: 5^2=Y, the 25th letter.
6	T	The position of the letter in the alphabet is obtained by multiplying together the two numbers that precede it: 4×5=T=20th letter.
7	1	In this sequence, the number of each letter in the alphabet is obtained by subtracting the two numbers that follow: H 8th letter = 9(−1).
8	O	Each letter corresponds to the first letter of that number when written down.

Test II

PROBLEM No.	SOLUTION	EXPLANATION

The Card Sequence

PROBLEM No.	SOLUTION	EXPLANATION
1	Ace of Hearts	Each card decreases by three, with all four suits represented.
2	Four of Diamonds	Each line has three suits, Spades, Diamonds, Clubs, in a different order. The right hand card is always obtained by subtracting the second card from the first: $9-2=7$, $10-5=5$, $6-2=(4)$.
3	Six of Diamonds inside; Three of Diamonds outside	All cards are Diamonds. Starting with the top ace and moving clockwise, alternating outside and inside, the sequence is 1, 2, (3), 4, 5. From the top Two of Diamonds, alternating inside-outside, the progression is 2, 4, (6), 8, 10, each number being obtained by adding two to the preceding one.
4	Ten of Clubs	The group of five Diamonds corresponds to a group of five Clubs. The number on the middle card of each group is equal to the numbers of the cards of the whole group added together: $1+3+3+2=9$ and $4+1+1+4=(10)$.

PROBLEM No.	SOLUTION	EXPLANATION
5	Ace of Diamonds	On each line, the cards have the same suit. In both the top group and the bottom group, the sum of the two diagonal cards is equal. $10+2=5+7$ and so $8+(1)=3+6$.
6	Ace of Hearts	On each line, the cards have the same suit. From the first line (top) to the fourth line (bottom), the numbers progression is $+2$: 2, 4 $(2+2)$, 6, 8 $(1+6+1)$.

The Domino Sequence

1	Double one	Working from top to bottom, left to right, the dominos increase by a double each time.
2	6/5	The top half of the right hand domino on each line is equal to the sum of the two top halves that precede it: $1+4=5$, $4+0=4$, $5+1=(6)$. The bottom halves of each domino decrease by one each time: 6, 5, 4, 3, 2, 1, 0, 6, (5).
3	3/1	The number 1 is present on each domino, alternating inside and outside. Starting with the bottom half of the top domino, and alternating outside-inside, the numbers decrease by one each time.

PROBLEM No.	SOLUTION	EXPLANATION
4	5/4	Starting from the top, the numbers on the dominos descend in simple numerical order with a six following a blank (zero) and a single number omitted before each domino: 2−1=6 −5=3 −2=4 −3=1 −0= (5−4).
5	1/6 and 6/2	The left hand sequence, from top to bottom, shows a decreasing progression where each value is separated from the preceding one by one: 4(3)2(1)0(6)5(4) 3(2)1(0)6(5)4(3)2(1)0(6)5(4) 3(2)*1*(0)*6*(5). The right hand sequence, from top to bottom, shows an increasing progression where each value is separated from the preceding one by alternately two and one: 4(5/6) 0(1) 2(3/4) 5(6) 0(1/2) 3(4) 5(6/0) 1(2) 3(4/5) 6(0) 1(2/3) 4(5) *6*(0/1) *2*.
6	2/4	The values of the left hand sides of the dominos, looked at from the centre, follow a progression of +2, −1: 1 is the second number after 6; 0 the first before 1; 2 the 2nd after 1, 1 the first before 2; 3 the 2nd after 1; (2) the first before 3. The values of the right hand sides of the dominos follow a progres-

PROBLEM No.	SOLUTION	EXPLANATION

sion of +1, +2, +3, +4, +5, +6: 5 is the 1st value after4; 0 the 2nd value after 5, 3 the 3rd value after 0, etc.

The Graphic Sequence

1	3	The line turns 45° each time.
2	6	The circle moves one place diagonally; the square one place horizontally.
3	5	The whole shape turns 90° each time.
4	3	The circle and square move clockwise, the circle changing colour each time. The triangle moves anti-clockwise.
5	4	All figures contain a semi-circle.
6	1	The top right hand square moves diagonally, the bottom left hand square moves horzontally.
7	2	The central line moves 45°. The circles moves along the line a quarter each time. The square moves sides and changes colour each time.
8	5	The stripes in the left hand side of the square move 45° anti-clockwise each time. The stripes in the right hand side of the square are alternately horizontal and vertical.

Are you logical?

Write your scores into the table below. This will give you an overall view of your results.

TEST I	TEST II
1 The Numbers Sequence (6 questions) Total of correct answers:	4 The Cards Sequence (6 questions) Total of correct answers:
2 The Letters Sequence (6 questions) Total of correct answers:	5 The Dominos Sequence (6 questions) Total of correct answers:
3 The Combined Sequence (8 questions) Total of correct answers:	6 The Graphics Sequence (8 questions) Total of correct answers:
Total questions: 40 Total correct answers:	

You can interpret these results in several ways: globally, as a whole; sequence by sequence; or by making certain comparisons.

Globally

This test is valid if your overall score is between 6 and 22 correct answers. If you have less than 6 or more than 22 correct answers, then something is wrong. It may be the test or it may be you. But whatever it is, it is abnormal. You are not made for this test or this test is not made for you.

- **Between 6 and 14 correct answers . . .**
  You are average. You follow a train of thought and have good sense. You reason well, but if you are closer to 6 then you lack rigour. On the other hand, if you are closer to 14 you have a good sense of abstraction.

- **Between 15 and 18 correct answers . . .**
  You have more than just good sense; a rigorous logical ability to analyse and excellent judgement. You are very coherent, even if sometimes you are slightly too precise in your reasoning.

- **Between 18 and 22 correct answers . . .**
  You have impeccable logic and an excellent degree of abstraction. You are very methodical in your thinking, even obsessional. You reason precisely and clearly, but sometimes lack that special 'spirit' that rounds off the sharp edges.

Sequence by Sequence

- You are **'weak'** in a given sequence if you have otained less than 2 points in sequences 1, 2, 4 and 5 or less than 3 points in sequences 3 and 6.

- You are **'strong'** in a given sequence if you have obtained more than 3 points in sequences 1, 2, 4 and 5 or more than 4 points in sequences 3 and 6.

By Comparison

Compare your results in sequences 1 and 2.

- If you have scored better in sequence 1, you are better at 'deduction' — reasoning from general rules to particular cases. If you have scored better in sequence 2, you are better at 'induction' — reasoning from particular examples to general rules.

  These results are obviously only indicative. It is very difficult to distinguish clearly between induction and deduction in tests, just as it is in reality.

- Compare the results you obtained in sequences 3 and 6. A better performance in sequence 3 implies a more 'conceptual' form of intelligence. You think more easily in words and have a good perception and comprehension of signs.

  More success in sequence 6 implies a more 'visual' form of intelligence. You think more easily in images: you are very perceptive when it comes to shapes.

THE NUMERICAL FACTOR

The numerical factor (Thurstone's N factor) is essential when it comes to evaluating intelligence. It relates to the area of superior intellectual functioning and one's ability to manipulate numbers. All tests that use numbers; reasoning tests for example (see previous chapter) are more or less saturated by this factor. The tests that give the best measure are the ones where the N factor is greatest, showing an ability in simple arithmetic: addition, subtraction, multiplication and division.

Contrary to the opinion often voiced by those who are no good at arithmetic, the ability to calculate is not a simple technical function. It reveals the basis of intelligence; an ability to resolve complex problems by carrying out simple operations.

The Test

The following test has been devised to allow you to better evaluate your ability to calculate. Problems are presented and you must decide whether the answers are correct by crossing the appropriate box.

You must do all calculations in your head without writing anything down or using a calculator. The tests lasts 15 minutes, on average, 25 seconds per problem. You do not, therefore, have time to get stuck on one particular problem. Of all the tests, this is the one where it is most important to cross all the boxes.

Here are some examples to familiarise you with the type of problem posed. You have as much time as you need.

Examples: problems

Is the total right?

1.	$66 + 31 = 97$	YES	NO
2.	$43 - 27 = 16$	YES	NO
3.	$28 \times 4 = 112$	YES	NO
4.	$\dfrac{43}{6} = 7$	YES	NO
5.	$2^6 = 66$	YES	NO
6.	$\dfrac{19 - 3 + 5 + 6 - 8}{7 + 4 - 10 + 18} = 1$	YES	NO

Examples: solutions

The answers for problems 4 and 5 are incorrect:
($43/6 = 7.166$ and $2^6 = 64$).

STOP: This is where the real test begins.
ATTENTION: You have 15 minutes and not a
second more.

Is the total right?

1.	$45 - 38 = 7$	YES	NO
2.	$53 + 48 = 103$	YES	NO
3.	$12 \times 24 = 288$	YES	NO
4.	$\dfrac{76}{6} = 13$	YES	NO
5.	$4^5 = 1024$	YES	NO
6.	$5 \times 12 = 15 \times 4$	YES	NO
7.	$\dfrac{360}{18} = 20$	YES	NO
8.	$4317 \times 3 = 12951$	YES	NO
9.	$728 + 452 = 1180$	YES	NO
10.	$913 - 357 = 555$	YES	NO
11.	$\dfrac{3^7}{7^3} = 6$	YES	NO
12.	$\dfrac{21}{42} = \dfrac{37}{73}$	YES	NO
13.	$8456 - 3457 = 4999$	YES	NO

Is the total right?

14.	$36 + 3 - 15 - 7 + 21 - 14 = 24$	YES	NO
15.	$(3 \times 7) - 11 - (6 \times 2) + 2 = 0$	YES	NO
16.	$\dfrac{581}{83} = 7$	YES	NO
17.	$\dfrac{8436}{703} = 13$	YES	NO
18.	$677 \times 11 = 7447$	YES	NO
19.	$4 + 8 - (7 \times 2) + 5 = 3$	YES	NO
20.	$\dfrac{(7 \times 3) - 19}{2 \times (5 - 4)} = 1$	YES	NO
21.	$3256 - 1327 = 2357 - 429$	YES	NO
22.	$67 \times 7 = 469$	YES	NO
23.	$76 \times 6 = 456$	YES	NO
24.	$455 + 545 = 1000$	YES	NO
25.	$333 - 333 = 0$	YES	NO
26.	$\dfrac{1311}{3} = 437$	YES	NO
27.	$4539 \times 7 = 31773$	YES	NO

28.
$$\begin{array}{r} 2327 \\ +7232 \\ \hline 9559 \end{array}$$
YES   NO

29.
$$\begin{array}{r} 6315 \\ +1728 \\ \hline 7033 \end{array}$$
YES   NO

30.
$$\begin{array}{r} 7623 \\ -6732 \\ \hline 1991 \end{array}$$
YES   NO

Is the total right?

31.
```
   8537
  −7804
   733
```
YES   NO

32. $\dfrac{86247}{777} = 111$ YES   NO

33.
```
   3513
 ×   45
  17565
  14052
 158085
```
YES   NO

34.
```
   9427
 ×   73
  28281
  65989
 688071
```
YES   NO

35.
```
    7613
 ×   327
   53291
   15226
   22839
 2489451
```
YES   NO

36. $\dfrac{108}{9} = 3^2 + 3$ YES   NO

37. $111^3 = 1367633$ YES   NO

38. $\dfrac{3149}{235} = 13.4$ YES   NO

39. $43 + 27 - 13 + 7 + 5$
$- 21 + 4 - 9 = 43$ YES   NO

40. $\dfrac{3888}{360} = 10.8$ YES   NO

Your Score

Each correct answer is worth one point, no matter how difficult the problem.

Check your answers with the table below and keep a total of correct answers.

Questions	Is the total right?	Questions	Is the total right?
1	YES	21	NO
2	NO	22	YES
3	YES	23	YES
4	NO	24	YES
5	YES	25	YES
6	YES	26	YES
7	YES	27	YES
8	YES	28	YES
9	YES	29	NO
10	NO	30	NO
11	No	31	YES
12	NO	32	YES
13	YES	33	YES
14	YES	34	NO
15	YES	35	YES
16	YES	36	YES
17	NO	37	NO
18	YES	38	YES
19	YES	39	YES
20	YES	40	YES

How to Interpret Your Results

• Between 6 and 9 correct answers
You are ill at ease with numbers and different arithmetic operations tend to irritate you. You have learned the basics but forgotten most of it through laziness or disinterest. Your ability to work with abstracts is low and you think more often in images.

• Between 10 and 18 correct answers
You are about average. You calculate well and have no need of a calculator to solve the small arithmetic problems of everyday life. If you are nearer 10, best check your change when it is given to you. Nearer 18 and you have a good level of mental agility when it comes to calculations.

• Between 19 and 27 correct answers
You have a very high ability to work with abstracts and a real ability to manipulate numbers. This is proof of a critical mind that is both efficient and precise. Whether you sacrificed precision for rapidity or not, these are excellent results and your intuition (or luck) has served you well.

• Between 28 and 32 correct answers
If you are not a chartered accountant or finalist in 'Countdown' these are exceptional results. But even if you have been trained in number manipulation for one reason or another, your results prove that you have a gift and a real talent for arithmetic.

THE MEMORY FACTOR

The memory factor concerns the psychic functions that give us the ability to remember the past, as it was. In reality, four distinct operations are used on a given piece of information.

1. Grasp (recording, fixation).

2. Conservation (saving, storing).

3. Recall (evaluation, reminiscence).

4. Recognition (identification, localisation).

The memory is a complex function. One should, for example, distinguish between evocation and reminiscence, identification and localisation.

Evocation is a voluntary effort of recalling the memory; reminiscence is, on the contrary, an involuntary recalling — a memory returning to your mind which is not recognised as such.

On the other hand, identification is the action of recognising something current as something from the past, and thus of establishing a memory as such; localisation implies relocating this memory in its time context.

On the intelligence map we must also distinguish another factor as well as the memory factor, called 'instant memory' which makes other intellectual mechanisms intervene. As opposed to what can properly be called past memory, instant memory is distinguished by there being no saving of information, or mnemonic fixation (to use computer language).

Immediate memory corresponds slightly to learning 'by heart'. Only slightly, because by learning something 'by heart' there is something that resembles habitual memory, a group of impressions that continue to influence our behaviour and responses.

The tests used to evaluate these two mnemonic capacities are obviously different. The first concerns grouping elements with no logical link between them; the second concerns sequences of numbers. We will begin with the latter.

Test your immediate memory

This test is composed of four tests, with each one containing seven sequences of numbers. You must read each sequence once and reconstitute it from memory. You may pause between each test. You should check your results for tests 1 and 2. Tests 3 and 4 are 'recap' tests.

Examples

a) **Read carefully each sequence of numbers once, then write them down again from memory.**

9....8....4
7....6....1....5
3....1....2....7....4

b) **Read carefully each sequence of numbers once, then write them down again, backwards, from memory.**

6....3....1
7....5....4....6
2....5....3....7....1

STOP:
THE TEST BEGINS HERE. HAVE YOU READ
THE INSTRUCTIONS WELL?

Test I

Read carefully the following sequence of numbers once, and write them out from memory.

3....6....4
1....2....5....3
5....1....4....9....7
5....3....1....2....8....7
4....1....7....6....3....1....7
5....7....3....1....8....6....9....4
7....1....3....2....6....8....5....4....9

Test II

Read carefully the following sequence of numbers once, and write them out in reverse order, from memory.

6....3....1
1....4....5....3
7....4....2....5....1
3....7....6....8....2....5
5....7....8....3....4....2....1
2....4....8....9....7....3....5....1
9....2....6....8....3....7....4....1....5

CHECK YOUR RESULTS

Check your results in these two tests. Note the amount of numbers you were able to recall from memory, both forwards and backwards. Try to do better in the following tests.

Test III

Read carefully the following sequence of numbers once, and write them out from memory.

3....6....5
1....7....4....2
5....8....9....7....1
4....1....3....9....7....6
2....7....9....4....6....3....5
9....8....3....1....5....2....7....4
7....4....8....5....3....9....6....2....1

Test IV

Read carefully the following sequence of numbers once and once only, then write them out in reverse order, from memory.

3....1....5
6....2....7....4
5....4....3....7....9
1....6....7....8....4....5
7....8....3....2....5....1....4
8....1....3....7....4....5....2....6
2....9....5....6....1....4....3....8....7

CHECK YOUR RESULTS

Check your results and note the amount of numbers you were able to recall from memory, both forwards and backwards. Compare your results with those of the last two tests and retain only your best score.

How to interpret your results

An adult incapable of repeating a sequence of five numbers in their correct order, or three numbers in reverse order, is considered as mentally deficient. This, therefore, is your minimum.

You are above average if you can recall between six and eight numbers in their correct order and between four and six numbers in reverse order.

You are extremely gifted or particularly well trained if you can recall nine numbers in their correct order, or between seven and nine numbers in reverse order.

Note

The normal procedure for this test involves a 'tester' and the subject involved (the person tested). The tester pronounces each sequence with a break of one second per number. The subject must repeat each sequence from memory.

Normally the numbers increase in their amount from three to nine. If the subject makes a mistake in a given sequence, the tester allows the subject to try and memorise the same amount of numbers as the previous sequence. If the subject succeeds, the test continues with the following sequence, if he fails, the test is over.

After a break, one continues with the next numbers sequences, where the subject must repeat the numbers in reverse order, starting with the last number mentioned.

You can ask a relative to test you because he or she will without doubt be more stringent.

This test is, however, not of great use to evaluate your overall memory, for the tests needed to do this are much more elaborate. On the following pages are tests that allow you to know if you have a good memory.

Test your memory

The following test has been devised to evaluate your overall memory and to appraise all the functions involved.

It is made up of seven tests. You must follow the instructions to the letter and check your results only when all the tests are finished.

Fetch a pencil and a rubber and look at the opposite page very carefully; memorise the words under each picture. Take your time to memorise them and then turn the page.

Note

These tests do not have a time limit. But if you haven't found the answers after two minutes you can go on to the next test.

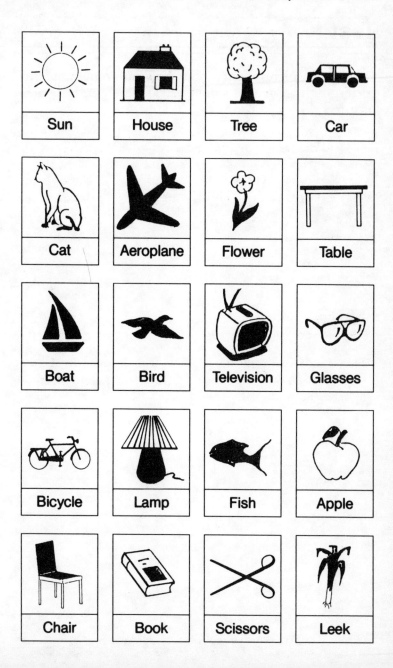

Test I

Here are the pictures once again. You must remember the corresponding names and write them under each picture.

Test II

The pictures opposite are extremely simplified. You must remember the corresponding names and write them under each picture.

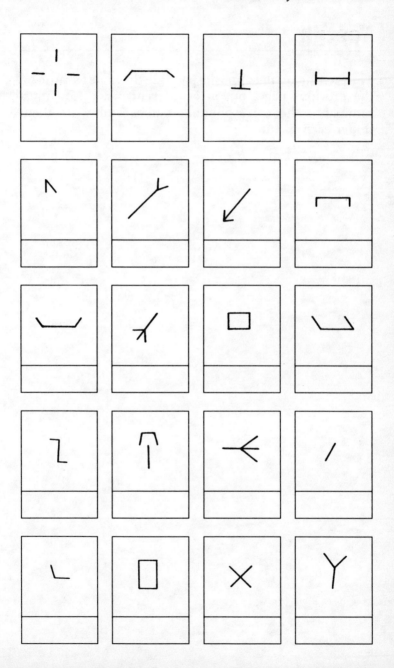

Test III

The pictures on the opposite page are the same as those on the previous page, but in a different order. You must remember the corresponding names and write them under each picture.

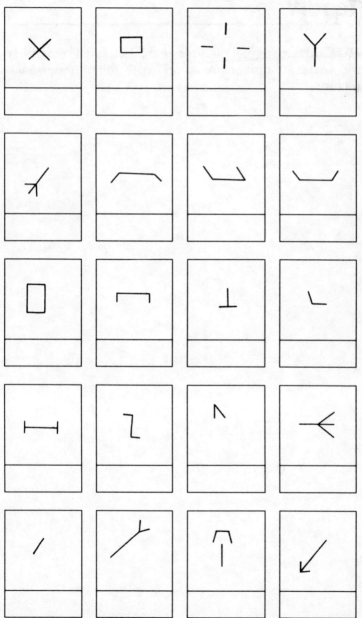

Test IV

Here are the original pictures again. You must remember the corresponding names and write them under each picture.

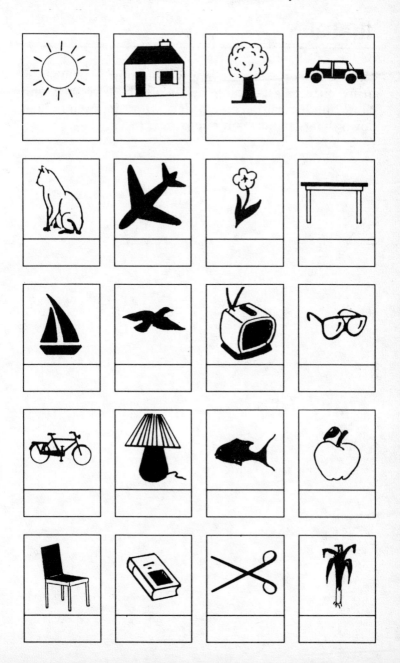

Test V

The squares opposite are empty. You must remember as many pictures as possible and write the corresponding names underneath. Their order is not important. Take down things as they come into your head.

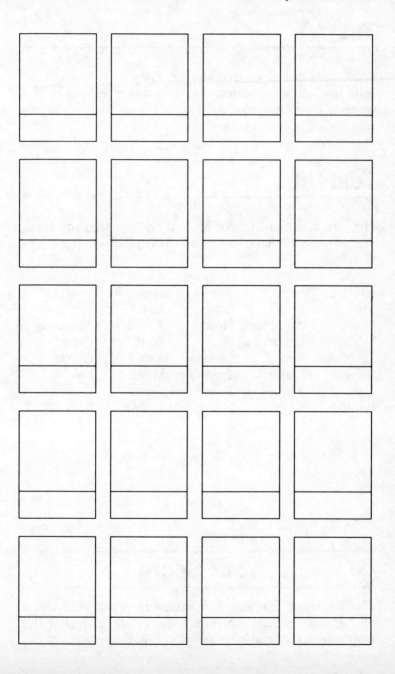

Test VI

Close the book or turn to another chapter. Occupy yourself for about 20 minutes, then take a pen and paper and write down the names of as many of the pictures as you can remember in two minutes.

Test VII

Here is a list of 40 words. You must underline from memory the 20 that correspond to the pictures on the previous pages.

Crab	Sun	Box	Armchair	House
Tree	Pencil	Car	Cat	Tie
Pear	Aeroplane	Flower	Radio	Ashtray
Table	Umbrella	Boat	Bird	Cigar
Television	Egg	Glasses	Knife	Chimney
Bicycle	Lamp	Trombone	Shoe	Key
Fish	Apple	Telephone	Chair	Carrot
Book	Scissors	Horse	Ladder	Leek

Your Score

Check your results (out of 20) for each test and keep a note of each correct answer. The answers are correct if the words are exact and/or correspond to the pictures in the correct order.

How to interpret your results

The memory exercise always ties in very much with other functions of intelligence: observation, imagination, language, to name but a few. But memory is also dependent on culture, practice and personality. Evaluating one's real abilities is, therefore, very difficult. You should interpret your performances with a certain amount of prudence, taking into account your form and age as well as you motivation when you took this test. Because just as one's abilities diminish with age, they also diminish in times of instability.

• Test I
This test allows one to judge immediate memory or recalling capabilities. The average amount of answers is about 8-9 out of 20.

• Test II
This test allows one to evaluate recognition faculties and spatial memory. The average is about 7-8 correct answers out of 20.

• Test III
This test allows one to judge 'raw' memory, irrespective of spatial memory. The average is normally less than in the preceding test (about 6-7 out of 20).

• Test IV
This test allows one to evaluate recall faculties; one's capacity to 'grasp' things. The average is normally greater than in the last two tests, and on a level with the first test.

•Test V
This test allows one to evaluate evocation faculties and voluntary memory. The average is normally the same as in of the preceding test.

144 / *Succeed at I.Q. Tests*

• Test VI
This takes past memory into account and one's conservation capacities, or evocative memory faculties. The
average is normally about the same as that of the preceding one.

• Test VII
This test concerns memory recognition and allows one to
evaluate identification faculties. The performance level is
normally close to 20.

From now on you are in a position to evaluate your
mnemonic capacities and your strengths and weaknesses
in the different mental activities that make up one's
memory.

Beware, however, of over-estimating good and bad performances. More often than not they are a sign that there is
something wrong with the test, rather than in your
head.

THE PERCEPTION FACTOR

Strictly speaking, perception is an ability of the mind to represent objects. Like the memory it plays a central role in psychological and mental activities.

The perception factor, dealt with in this chapter, is restricted to a visual domain. It is the ability to discover a specified configuration within a more complex configuration.

The tests that allow this aptitude to be evaluated are discrimination tests. They involve recognising identical or different shapes and figures. We propose two.

Test I

The test is made up of a series of ten pairs of seemingly identical configurations.

You must find the small detail that differentiates the second of each pair from the first. You have six minutes to do them, or just under 40 seconds per pair. You don't have time, therefore, to spend too long on one particular pair. If you cannot find the difference within a reasonable period of time, move on to the next pair.

1

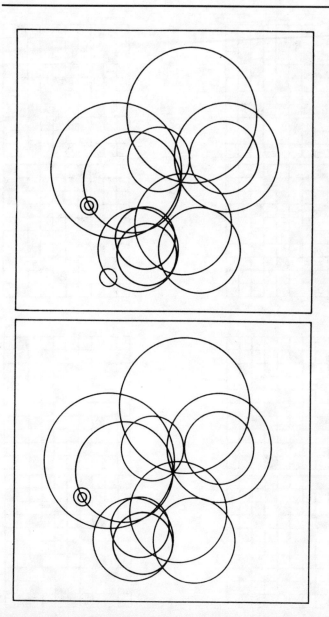

II

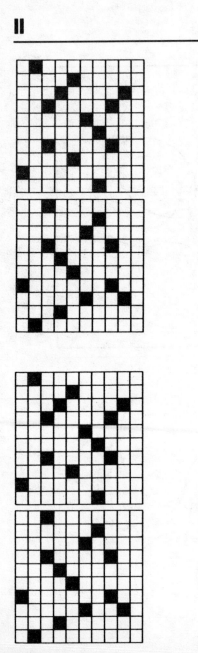

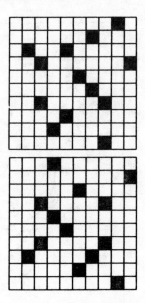

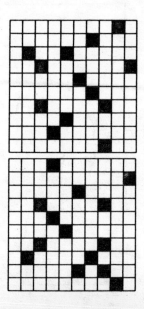

III

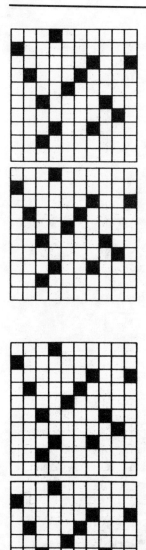

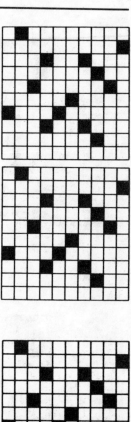

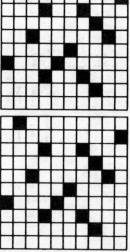

IV

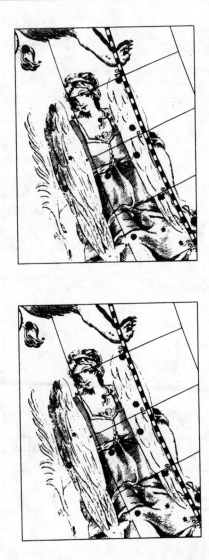

V

VI

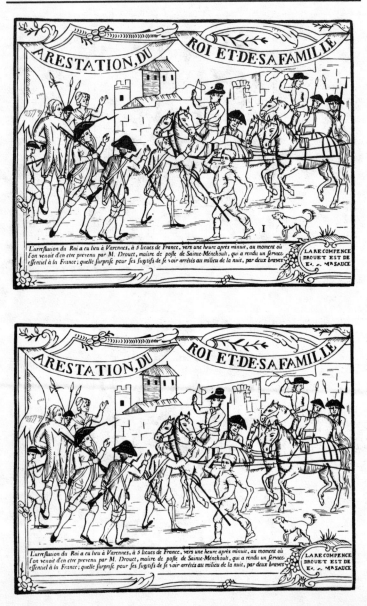

VII

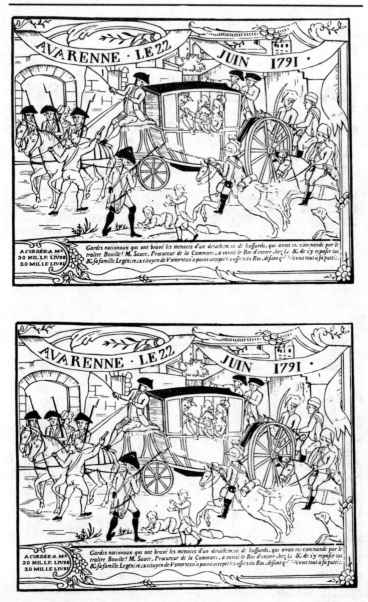

VIII

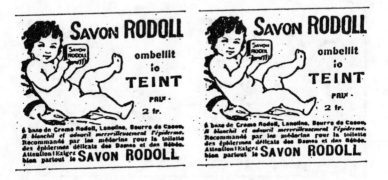

IX

X

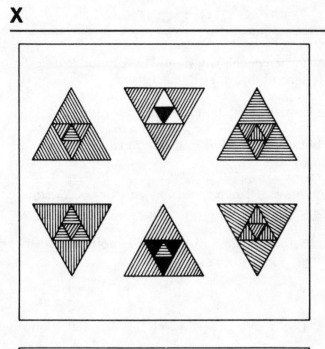

Your Score

Here are the ten details you should have found to differentiate the second drawings in each pair:

I: a small circle at the bottom left is missing.

II: the bottom right hand grid has an extra black square (bottom right).

III: the bottom left hand grid has an extra black square (bottom left).

IV: the thumb on the right hand that holds the feather is missing.

V: a star is missing on the left knee.

VI: the 1 is missing to the left of the dog (bottom right).

VII: the bayonet of the centre soldier on the left has disappeared.

VIII: one of the 'L's' of Rodoll is missing on the soap in the child's hands.

IX: the opener is missing at the top of the bottle on the cap.

X: the stripes are inverted inside the little triangle at the bottom right.

Your score is equal to the number of correct answers, minus any wrong or unanswered problems. This gives you a score of between −10 and +10. Write down your score; you will need it a little later.

Test II

This test consists of four sets of 25 questions. Each set is made up of a list of pairs of numbers or words written out in two columns. You must point out which pairs are identical and which are or different, and all this in four minutes.

Examples: questions

Test 1 / Ring the identical pairs

a.	4335	4353
b.	345628	345628
c.	765098	765098
d.	95647.94	96547.94
e.	4356.435	4356.435
f.	768423	768423

Test 2 / Ring the different pairs

a.	47689	47689
b.	54345654	54345456
c.	76587645	76587645
d.	453985764	543985764
e.	23981274653	2398124563
f.	345264	345264
g.	456391	465391

Test 3 / Ring the identical pairs:

a. Scott Fitzgerald   Scott Fitzgerald
b. Giuseppe Garibaldi   Giusepe Garibaldi
c. Republic of Maldives   Republic of Maldines
d. William Ewart Gladstone   William Ewart Gladstone
e. Cornelius Vanderbilt   Cornelious Vanderbilt

Test 4 / Ring the different pairs:

a. Laurel & Hardy   Laurel and Hardy
b. Gabriele Sabatini   Gabriela Sabatini
c. Lyndon Baines Johnson   Lyndon Baines Johnstone
d. Newcastle upon Tyne   Newcastle upon Tyne
e. Siegfried Sassoon   Siegfried Sassoon

Examples: answers

You should have ringed the following lines:
- Test 1: b, c, e, f
- Test 2: b, d, e, g
- Test 3: a, d
- Test 4: a, b, c

ATTENTION: This is where the real test begins.

You have 4 minutes and not a second more.

Set I

Ring the identical pairs:

1.	3478	3478
2.	63127	63127
3.	564789	564789
4.	2334589	2384589
5.	16781134	16781134
6.	113411891178	113411891178
7.	5777111823111978	5777111823111978
8.	134675115773449	134675115773449
9.	134656489987	13456489987
10.	683397	683397
11.	7214321	7214321
12.	5632147	5632147
13.	2673899	2673899
14.	2623989	2623989
15.	52146775	52146775
16.	88977898	88977898
17.	64325	64325
18.	76113	76113
19.	76224	76224
20.	89112532	89112532
21.	14183945	14183645
22.	13211729	13211729
23.	574319	574319
24.	28121821	28121821
25.	47388374	47388374

Set II

Ring the different pairs:

1.	362416	362416
2.	377344	377344
3.	9813269	9318269
4.	14273	14273
5.	63646569	63646569
6.	123456798	123456798
7.	324472573	324472573
8.	018899372573	018899372573
9.	20849	20849
10.	19881989	19881989
11.	6124578312	6124573812
12.	34273829	34273829
13.	73489315	73489315
14.	78119824	78119824
15.	3265142213	3295142213
16.	472483912	472483192
17.	172834	172834
18.	963451	963451
19.	38245516	38245516
20.	172137	172137
21.	18324625	18324625
22.	11261315	11261315
23.	101010110001111	101010110001111
24.	0110110101101	0110110101101
25.	1101101010	1101101010

Set III

Ring the identical pairs:

1.	Benjamin Franklin	Benjamin Franklin
2.	The Hellenic Republic	The Hellenic Republic
3.	Samuel Taylor Coleridge	Samuel Taylor Coleridge
4.	Richard Milhous Nixon	Richard Milhous Nixon
5.	Anatoliy Karpov	Anatoliy Karpov
6.	Sir Mohammed Iqbal	Sir Mohammed Iqubal
7.	Liechtenstein	Liechtenstein
8.	Republic of Paraguay	Republic of Paraguey
9.	Otto Preminger	Otto Preminger
10.	Napoleon Bonaparte	Napoleon Bonaparte
11.	Paul Henri Spaak	Paul Henri Spaak
12.	Tannhäuser	Tannhäuser
13.	Piscis Austrinus	Piscis Austrinus
14.	Humboldt's Sea	Humboldt's Sea
15.	Penelope Lively	Penelope Lively
16.	Thomas Aquinas	Thomas Aquinas
17.	Paul Cézanne	Paul Cezanne
18.	Saskatchewan	Saskatchawen
19.	Willy Brandt	Willy Brandt
20.	Mt. Kilimanjaro	Mt. Kilimanjaro
21.	Richard Attenborough	Richard Attenborough
22.	Larry McMurtry	Larry MacMurtry
23.	Evander Holyfield	Evander Holyfield
24.	Kenneth A. Russell	Kenneth A. Russell
25.	Guatemala	Guatemala

Set IV

Ring the different pairs:

1. Jack Nicholson — Jack Nicholson
2. James Callaghan — James Callaghan
3. Alpha Centauri — Alpha Centauri
4. Guinea-Bissau — Guinea Bissau
5. Helmut Schmidt — Helmut Scmhidt
6. Lake Titicaca — Lake Titicaca
7. Czechoslovakia — Czechoslovakia
8. Sir Alfred Hitchcock — Sir Alfred Hitchcock
9. Solicitor-General — Solicitor-General
10. Francesco Zuccarelli — Francesco Zuccarrelli
11. Robert Gabriel Mugabe — Robert Gabriel Mugabe
12. Tyrrhenian Sea — Tyrrhenian Sea
13. Sao Tomé — Sao Tomé
14. Tadzhikistan — Tadzhikistan
15. Luxembourg — Luxembourg
16. Spiro T. Agnew — Spiro T. Agnew
17. Gaelic Football — Gaelic Football
18. Boris Yeltsin — Boris Yeltsin
19. Timbuktu — Timbuckto
20. Joseph Pulitzer — Joseph Pulitzer
21. Sir Charles Wheatstone — Sir Charles Wheatstone
22. Philip J. Carter — Philip J. Carter
23. Martina Navratilova — Martina Navratilova
24. Vaslav Nijinsky — Vaslav Nijinsky
25. Anwar El-Sadat — Anwar El-Sedat

Your Score

You should have:

Set I: Ringed all pairs except 4, 9, 21.

Set II: Ringed pairs 3, 11, 15, 16.

Set III: Ringed all pairs except 6, 8, 17, 18, 22.

Set IV: Ringed pairs 4, 5, 10, 19, 25.

Once again, your score equals the number of correct answers, minus the number of wrong answers or unanswered questions.

Divide by 10 and once again you have a number between −10 and +10.

How to interpret your results

You will have a good indication of your performance level by taking the number of correct answers from the two preceding tests and the number of wrong answers, or non-replies.

Write your results into the grid below to have a better overall view.

	Correct Answers	Wrong Answers	Non-replies	
Set 1				
Set 2				
Set 3				
Set 4				
Test I (from page 156)				SCORE* 1
Test II				SCORE** 2
				AVERAGE ***

* Number of correct answers — no false answers — no non-replies.
** Number of correct answers — no false answers — no non-replies.
*** Score 1 plus Score 2 divided by two.

- **Your average is equal to or less than −2.**
This is fairly unlikely; an under par, or very tired, performance perhaps: the sign of a state of mind that lacks discrimination.

- **Your average is between −1 and +2.**
This is fairly normal. You have good perceptive speed and do not lack discrimination.

- **Your average is between +3 and +6.**
This is excellent. You are attentive, quick and precise; you understand things clearly. You are good at judging what is true and what is false and spotting variations.

- **Your average is equal or greater than +7.**
This is rare and unlikely. You must have mistaken your score somewhere, or perhaps you have not strictly followed the procedure. This is more likely than such a high performance level.

- **You have scored higher in Test 1.**
You have a better perception of shapes than relationships, a more global approach with good powers of observation.

- **You have scored higher in Test 2.**
You have a better perception of relationships than shapes, of parts than of the whole. You have a more analytical mind and a certain talent for making comparisons.

- **You gave more wrong answers than non-replies.**
You lack precision due to carelessness if you have made more mistakes in the last two tests than the first two, and you find it difficult to concentrate if the number of errors you made is the same in all tests.

• **You gave more non-replies than wrong answers.**
You lack speed, which is due either to difficulty in
performance, if your non-replies are spread evenly
through each test, or a weakening perception, if you have
accumulated your non-replies at the end of the test.

THE VERBAL FACTOR

Man is a speaking being, and there is no intelligence without language.

Thurstone's V factor refers to an essential ability. This ability, which plays a central role in success at school, has a unique place amongst all the others.

All the abilities we describe are essential to intelligence but verbal understanding is even more so. Without it, none of the others can be taken in, described or evaluated.

The verbal factor is of such importance because it is at the heart of all expression and communication.

The tests used to evaluate comprehension are very numerous. The problem with this type of test is in avoiding:

•   Subjective references, in which case it is no longer an intelligence test, but a personality test. Asking, for example, in a test whether 'in case of danger, everyone's for himself' is of the same or more significance than 'need prevails' shows less about the subject's good sense (or common sense) than his judgement of values.

- Particular references, for this would make it a test of understanding rather than an intelligence test. For example, this would be the case in tests where the vocabulary refers to technical matters that can only be acquired by knowledge of a specialised area.

The ones we propose; vocabulary tests, synonyms, antonyms, comprehension or analogy rest within the boundaries of everyday language and 'good sense'.

Test Your Comprehension Capacities

This test is made up of 60 problems, modelled on the following five examples. You must indicate which is the correct answer each time. Obviously you cannot use a dictionary or anything else to help you. There is no time limit to the test.

Examples: problems

1. **What is a thesaurus?**

   a. a small animal
   b. a book of words
   c. an type of dinosaur
   d. a political speech

2. **What is the synonym of 'acclimatise'?**

   equip, desert, accustom, accredit, transfer, redeem.

3. **What is the odd one out?**

   well-stocked, garnished, plump, flat, full, bushy.

4. **What is the opposite of 'exotic'?**

   eclectic, indigenous, erotic, endogenous, emphatic, homogenous.

5. **Streets are to the town, what roads are to the . . .**

   countryside, map, car, motorway.

Examples: solutions

1. A thesaurus is a book of words.
2. The synonym of 'acclimatise' is 'accustom'.
3. The odd one out is 'flat', which does not express the idea of 'abundance'.
4. The opposite of 'exotic' is 'indigenous'.
5. Streets are to the town what roads are to the countryside.

> **STOP:** THE TEST STARTS HERE.
> HAVE YOU UNDERSTOOD THE PRECEDING
> EXAMPLES?

---

1. **What is an adage?**

   a. a musical piece
   b. a man who does not look his age
   c. a traditional maxim
   d. a pocket agenda

2. **What is the synonym of 'fertile'?**

   futile, fecund, feverish, festive, leafy, easy

3. **What is the odd one out?**

   abolish, soften, weaken, deaden, supple, cool.

4. **What is the opposite of 'implicit'?**

   illicit, fortuitous, explicit, gratuitous, tacit, induced.

5. **Television is to the image what radio is to ...**

   music, the sound, speech, noise.

6. What is an edifice?

   a. a building
   b. an image
   c. an opening
   d. a white alpine plant

7. What is the synonym of 'intentionally'?

cleverly, seriously, differently, voluntarily, incidentally, sensibly.

8. What is the odd one out?

pretence, make believe, sinecure, trickery, deceit, fraud.

9. What is the opposite of 'common'?

crucial, great, normal, original, trivial, special.

10. Fire is to the chimney what fish are to the ...

fry, aquarium, fishmonger's, river.

11. What is a 'racket'?

   a. a set of teeth on a wheel
   b. an investigative exercise
   c. a noisy disorder
   d. a type of sports bat

12. What is the synonym of 'ethical'?

moral, skeletal, racial, alcoholic, ethereal, ascetic.

13. What is the odd one out?

apricot, cherry, peach, orange, avocado pear, medlar.

14. What is the opposite of 'sceptical'?

contagious, credulous, litigious, unique, infectious, unfaithful.

15. Time is to the stop-watch what pressure is to the . . .

thermometer, altimeter, barometer, hygrometer, pedometer, anemometer.

16. What is a 'schedule'?

a. an orthodox rite
b. a Roman ship
c. a cream maker
d. a timetable

17. What is the synonym of 'regress'?

reject, degrease, disgorge, recede, slim down, regret.

18. What is the odd one out?

clammy, slimy, viscous, graceful, syrupy, sugary.

19. What is the opposite of 'specious'?

spacious, special, serious, spatial, serial, spiral.

20. Horse is to chestnut as cat is to . . .

mint, milk, drink, canary

21. What is a 'sinecure'?

a. a Chinese chain
b. a treatment for sinusitis
c. a resort for cinema enthusiasts
d. a highly paid but easy job

22. What is the synonym of 'worn'?

trapped, pillaged, used, scoured, broken, erased.

23. What is the odd one out?

towel, diamond, light, gauntlet.

24. What is the opposite of 'monologue'?

analogue, apologue, dialogue, epilogue, homologue, prologue.

25. The word is to the sentence what the letter is to . . .

mind, word, writing, noun, alphabet, number.

26. What is a 'monolith'?

a. an aeroplane
b. a stone monument
c. a single eye-glass
d. a short book

27. What is the synonym of 'prodigal'?

considerable, surprising, extraordinary, lavish, wonderful, repentant, surprising.

28. What is the odd one out?

hemp, cotton, jute, flax, raffia, silk.

29. What is the opposite of 'voluble'?

apathetic, undecided, inert, pusillanimous, silent, impulsive.

30. Ivory is to the elephant what shell is to the . . .

necklace, tortoise, fish, snake.

31. What is a 'snack'.

a. a small cut
b. a light meal
c. a slap
d. a heap

32. What is the synonym of 'orthodox'?

contrary, contradictory, in conformity, debatable, contingent, appropriate.

33. What is the odd one out?

crab, shrimp, crayfish, lobster, crawfish, scampi.

34. What is the opposite of 'hardly'?

rarely, a lot, little, poorly, never, quickly.

35. Sweetness is to salt what dryness is to . . .

heat, cold, water, sourness, softness, hardness.

36. What is a 'seminar'?

a. a bag of sperm
b. a semi-annual magazine
c. a work meeting
d. a bracelet with seven rings

37. What is the synonym of 'verification'?

reconstruction, rebuilding, renovation, repair, restoration, proof.

38. What is the odd one out?

parabola, parachute, parados, umbrella, draught screen.

39. What is the opposite of 'blended'?

coloured, contrasted, varied, mottled, variegated, mixed.

40. The calf is to the cow what the chick is to the . . .

pullet, capon, hen, cockerel, poulard, cock.

41. What is a 'mediator'?

a. a professional of the media
b. a median plane
c. a conciliator
d. a TV personality

42. What is the synonym of 'incomprehensible'?

inexpressible, ineffable, indescribable, inexplicable, unrepeatable.

43. What is the odd one out?

competence, content, cubage, cubic capacity, tonnage, volume.

44. What is the opposite of 'innate'?

instinctive, atavistic, acquired, natural, hereditary, native.

45. Silence is to gold what speech is to ...

lead, tin, bronze, silver, platinum, steel.

46. What is a 'stereotype'?

a. a text in note form
b. a fixed opinion
c. a raised relief map
d. a stereo recording

47. What is the synonym of 'ostensible'?

uncertain, audacious, constructed, apparent, rigorous, true.

48. What is the odd one out?

lawn, parvis, pasture, prairie, field.

49. What is the opposite of 'sectarian'?

public, liberal, partisan, laic, nomad, regular.

50. The microscope is to the infinitely small what the telescope is to the inifintely ...

big, far, high, close, heavy, low.

51. What is 'anorexia'?

a. an exception to the rule
b. a weakening of smell
c. the absence of organs
d. a loss of appetite

52. What is the synonym of 'imminent'?

fatal, ineluctable, inevitable, infallible, necessary, close.

53. What is the odd one out?

double-bass, guitar, harp, mandolin, saxophone, violin.

54. What is the opposite of 'emit'?

deprive, assemble, omit, receive, deliver, decline.

55. The square is to the area what the cube is to the ...

weight, volume, depth, power, root, pressure.

56. What is a 'corollary'?

a. the solar crown
b. a direct consequence
c. the heart artery
d. the petals of a flower

57. What is the synonym of 'homogeneous'?

composite, equivocal, heteroclite, inverted, uniform, symmetrical.

58. What is the odd one out?

belote, bridge, canasta, queen, poker, tarot.

59. What is the opposite of 'rudimentary'?

elementary, refined, developed, soft, reassuring, pale.

60. The substance is to the form what the mind is to the ...

flesh, idea, letter, area, depth, imagination.

Your Score

Each correct answer is worth one point, but you must keep two different scores: one for the even-numbered questions, one for the odd-numbered questions. Your score is the average of these two scores; obviously it will be between 0 and 30.

Compare your answers with the following list:

1. An 'adage' is a traditional maxim.
2. The synonym of 'fertile' is 'fecund'.
3. The odd one out is 'abolish' which does not express the idea of moderation.
4. The opposite of 'implicit' is 'explicit'.
5. Television is to the image what radio is to the sound.
6. An 'edifice' is a building.
7. The synonym of 'intentionally' is 'voluntarily'.
8. The odd one out is 'sinecure', which does not express the idea of ruse or scheme.
9. The opposite of 'common' is 'original'.
10. Fire is to the chimney what fish are to the aquarium.
11. A 'racket' is a noisy disorder.
12. The synonym of 'ethical' is 'moral'.
13. The orange is not a fruit with a stone.
14. The opposite of 'sceptical' is 'credulous'.
15. Time is to the stop-watch what pressure is to the barometer.
16. A schedule is a timetable.
17. The synonym of 'regress' is 'recede'.
18. The odd one out is 'graceful'. All the others convey the idea of stickiness.
19. The opposite of 'specious' is 'serious'.
20. Horse is to chestnut as cat is to mint.
21. A 'sinecure' is a highly paid but easy job.
22. The synonym of 'worn' is 'used'.
23. Diamond. All the other words are parts of expressions using the verb 'throw'.
24. The opposite of 'monologue' is 'dialogue'.

25. The word is to the sentence what the letter is to the word.
26. A monolith is a stone monument.
27. The synonym of 'prodigal' is 'lavish'.
28. Silk is the only one which does not have a vegetable origin.
29. The opposite of 'voluble' is 'silent'.
30. Ivory is to the elephant what shell is to the tortoise.
31. A 'snack' is a light meal.
32. The synonym of 'orthodox' is 'in conformity'.
33. The crayfish is the only one which does not live in sea water.
34. The opposite of 'hardly' is 'a lot'.
35. Sweetness is to salt what dryness is to water.
36. A 'seminar' is a work meeting.
37. The synonym of 'verification' is 'proof'.
38. Parabola. All the others give the idea of protection.
39. The opposite of 'blended' is 'contrasted'.
40. The calf is to the cow what the chick is to the hen.
41. A 'mediator' is a 'conciliator'.
42. The synonym of 'incomprehensible' is 'inexplicable'.
43. 'Competence' is the only word which expresses a quality.
44. The opposite of 'innate' is 'acquired'.
45. Silence is to gold what speech is to silver.
46. A 'stereotype' is a fixed opinion.
47. The synonym of 'ostensible' is 'apparent'.
48. 'Parvis' is the only word of the series which does not imply an area of greenery.
49. The opposite of 'sectarian' is 'liberal'.
50. The microscope is to the infinitely small what the telescope is to the infinitely far.
51. 'Anorexia' is a loss of appetite.
52. The synonym of 'imminent' is 'close'.
53. Saxophone. All the others are string instruments.
54. The opposite of 'emit' is 'receive'.
55. The square is to the area what the cube is to the volume.
56. A 'corollary' is a direct consequence.
57. The synonym of 'homogeneous' is 'uniform'.
58. The odd one out is 'queen' as all the other words are card games.
59. The opposite of 'rudimentary' is 'developed'.
60. The substance is to the form what the mind is to the letter.

How to Interpret Your Results

You have made an average of your correct answers from the odd and even numbered questions. Your score is between 0 and 30.

- **If you have obtained less than 12 points.**
  Your comprehension capacities are quite weak; you lack vocabulary. You are more intuitive than rational and this might hinder you in your professional and social life. You often lack words when it comes to expressing your ideas clearly, and you often make false interpretations.

- **Between 13 and 22 points**
  You are amongst the average — upper average above 17 points, lower average below.
  You have a good level of understanding when it comes to expressing yourself and making yourself understood.
  But your intelligence is often more practical than conceptual. You don't always use words in their right sense and in an objective manner.

- **You have scored more than 22 points**
  You have excellent comprehension capacities and a very good level of understanding. You have no difficulty assimilating things and understanding what they mean. You express yourself and communicate your ideas with ease.

You should now have a fairly good idea of your comprehension faculties. But you must still measure your vocabulary level in order to appreciate your verbal capacities as a whole.

THE LEXICAL FACTOR

The lexical factor, like the verbal factor is, essential to intelligence because of the way it controls and operates language structure.

Thurstone's V factor refers to verbal comprehension and common sense ability (see previous chapter).

Thurstone's W (word) factor (verbal fluency) on the other hand concerns, the capacity to find the right words. It is the ability to produce words rapidly with an automatic check on the number or position of letters, the prefixes or the rhymes.

Test Your Verbal Fluency

The following test is based on models that allow you to evaluate your vocabulary level. It comprises 40 problems that you must solve within 30 minutes, which is less than one minute per problem. First, here are a few examples.

Examples: problems

1. Give 12 three letter words.

   1)   2)   3)
   4)   5)   6)
   7)   8)   9)
  10)   11)   12)

2. Give 12 words beginning with ACC.

   1) Acc.......   2) Acc.......   3) Acc.......
   4) Acc.......   5) Acc.......   6) Acc.......
   7) Acc.......   8) Acc.......   9) Acc.......
  10) Acc....... 11) Acc....... 12) Acc.......

3. Give 12 words finishing with TTLE:

   1) ....ttle   2) ....ttle   3) ....ttle
   4) ....ttle   5) ....ttle   6) ....ttle
   7) ....ttle   8) ....ttle   9) ....ttle
  10) ....ttle 11) ....ttle 12) ....ttle

4. Give 12 words beginning and finishing with the letter A:

1) A......a	2) A......a	3) A......a
4) A......a	5) A......a	6) A......a
7) A......a	8) A......a	9) A......a
10) A......a	11) A......a	12) A......a

Examples: answers

1. You have the choice of many common words, for example: *ace, bag, can, den, eat, fan, got, has, inn, jet, kin, law.*

2. There are over 30 without using variations, for example: *accept, accent, access, accident, acclaim, accolade, accommodate, accomplish, accord, accost, account, accrue.*

3. You may have any word found in the dictionary, for example: *battle, prattle, tattle, rattle, cattle, nettle, settle, kettle, mettle, shuttle, scuttle, little.*

4. There are plenty to choose from, for example: *aria, area, aroma, arena, armada, azalea, agenda, algebra, amenesia, ambrosia, aurora, aura.*

STOP.
THIS IS WHERE THE REAL TEST BEGINS.
HAVE YOU READ THE INSTRUCTIONS WELL?

If so, you may begin. You have 30 minuts and not a second more. Obviously, you may not use a dictionary or anything else to help you. You may use proper nouns, verbs, plurals or hyphenated words.

1. Find 12 four letter words:

1)	2)	3)
4)	5)	6)
7)	8)	9)
10)	11)	12)

2. Find 12 words beginning with PRO:

1) Pro......	2) Pro......	3) Pro......
4) Pro......	5) Pro......	6) Pro......
7) Pro......	8) Pro......	9) Pro......
10) Pro......	11) Pro......	12) Pro......

3. Find 12 words finishing with ENT:

1) ......ent	2) ......ent	3) ......ent
4) ......ent	5) ......ent	6) ......ent
7) ......ent	8) ......ent	9) ......ent
10) ......ent	11) ......ent	12) ......ent

4. Find 12 words that begin and end with the letter E:

1) E......e	2) E......e	3) E......e
4) E......e	5) E......e	6) E......e
7) E......e	8) E......e	9) E......e
10) E......e	11) E......e	12) E......e

5. Find 12 five letter words:

1)	2)	3)
4)	5)	6)
7)	8)	9)
10)	11)	12)

6. **Find 12 words beginning with EX:**

    1) Ex. . . . . . .   2) Ex. . . . . . .   3) Ex. . . . . . .
    4) Ex. . . . . . .   5) Ex. . . . . . .   6) Ex. . . . . . .
    7) Ex. . . . . . .   8) Ex. . . . . . .   9) Ex. . . . . . .
    10) Ex. . . . . . .   11) Ex. . . . . . .   12) Ex. . . . . . .

7. **Find 12 words ending in AIN:**

    1) . . . . . . .ain   2) . . . . . . .ain   3) . . . . . . .ain
    4) . . . . . . .ain   5) . . . . . . .ain   6) . . . . . . .ain
    7) . . . . . . .ain   8) . . . . . . .ain   9) . . . . . . .ain
    10) . . . . . . .ain   11) . . . . . . .ain 12) . . . . . . .ain

8. **Find 12 words that begin and end with the letter T:**

    1) T. . . . . . .t   2) T. . . . . . .t   3) T. . . . . . .t
    4) T. . . . . . .t   5) T. . . . . . .t   6) T. . . . . . .t
    7) T. . . . . . .t   8) T. . . . . . .t   9) T. . . . . . .t
    10) T. . . . . . .t   11) T. . . . . . .t 12) T. . . . . . .t

9. **Find 12 six letter words:**

    1)   2)   3)
    4)   5)   6)
    7)   8)   9)
    10)   11)   12)

10. **Find 12 words beginning with IM:**

    1) Im. . . . . . .   2) Im. . . . . . .   3) Im. . . . . . .
    4) Im. . . . . . .   5) Im. . . . . . .   6) Im. . . . . . .
    7) Im. . . . . . .   8) Im. . . . . . .   9) Im. . . . . . .
    10) Im. . . . . . .   11) Im. . . . . . . 12) Im. . . . . . .

11. **Find 12 words finishing with ECT:**

    1) . . . . . . .ect   2) . . . . . . .ect   3) . . . . . . .ect
    4) . . . . . . .ect   5) . . . . . . .ect   6) . . . . . . .ect
    7) . . . . . . .ect   8) . . . . . . .ect   9) . . . . . . .ect
    10) . . . . . . .ect 11) . . . . . . .ect 12) . . . . . . .ect

12. Find 12 words beginning and ending with the letter L:

1) L.......l   2) L.......l   3) L.......l
4) L.......l   5) L.......l   6) L.......l
7) L.......l   8) L.......l   9) L.......l
10) L.......l   11) L.......l   12) L.......l

13. Find 12 seven letter words:

1)   2)   3)
4)   5)   6)
7)   8)   9)
10)   11)   12)

14. Find 12 words beginning with TRANS:

1) Trans.....   2) Trans.....   3) Trans.....
4) Trans.....   5) Trans.....   6) Trans.....
7) Trans.....   8) Trans.....   9) Trans.....
10) Trans.....   11) Trans.....   12) Trans.....

15 Find 12 words ending in URE:

1) ......ure   2) ......ure   3) ......ure
4) ......ure   5) ......ure   6) ......ure
7) ......ure   8) ......ure   9) ......ure
10) ......ure   11) ......ure   12) ......ure

16. Find 12 words beginning ane ending in H:

1) H.......h   2) H.......h   3) H.......h
4) H.......h   5) H.......h   6) H.......h
7) H.......h   8) H.......h   9) H.......h
10) H.......h   11) H.......h   12) H.......h

17. Find 12 eight letter words:

1)   2)   3)
4)   5)   6)
7)   8)   9)
10)   11)   12)

18. Find 12 words beginning with COM:

1) Com.....	2) Com.....	3) Com.....
4) Com.....	5) Com.....	6) Com.....
7) Com.....	8) Com.....	9) Com.....
10) Com.....	11) Com.....	12) Com.....

19. Find 12 words ending in ION:

1) ......ion	2) ......ion	3) ......ion
4) ......ion	5) ......ion	6) ......ion
7) ......ion	8) ......ion	9) ......ion
10) ......ion	11) ......ion	12) ......ion

20. Find 12 words beginning and ending in D:

1) D......d	2) D......d	3) D......d
4) D......d	5) D......d	6) D......d
7) D......d	8) D......d	9) D......d
10) D......d	11) D......d	12) D......d

21. Find 12 nine letter words:

1)	2)	3)
4)	5)	6)
7)	8)	9)
10)	11)	12)

22. Find 12 words beginning in PRE:

1) Pre.....	2) Pre.....	3) Pre.....
4) Pre.....	5) Pre.....	6) Pre.....
7) Pre.....	8) Pre.....	9) Pre.....
10) Pre.....	11) Pre.....	12) Pre.....

23. Find 12 words ending in OR:

1) ......or	2) ......or	3) ......or
4) ......or	5) ......or	6) ......or
7) ......or	8) ......or	9) ......or
10) ......or	11) ......or	12) ......or

24. Find 12 words beginning and ending in N:

1) N . . . . . . n   2) N . . . . . . n   3) N . . . . n
4) N . . . . . n   5) N . . . . . . n   6) N . . . . . . n
7) N . . . . . n   8) N . . . . . . n   9) N . . . . . . n
10) N . . . . . . n   11) N . . . . . n   12) N . . . . . . n

25. Find 12 ten letter words.

1)   2)   3)
4)   5)   6)
7)   8)   9)
10)   11)   12)

26. Find 12 words beginning with BI:

1) Bi . . . . . .   2) Bi . . . . . .   3) Bi . . . . . .
4) Bi . . . . . .   5) Bi . . . . . .   6) Bi . . . . . .
7) Bi . . . . . .   8) Bi . . . . . .   9) Bi . . . . . .
10) Bi . . . . . .   11) Bi . . . . . .   12) Bi . . . . . .

27. Find 12 words ending in TER:

1) . . . . . . ter   2) . . . . . . ter   3) . . . . . . ter
4) . . . . . . ter   5) . . . . . . ter   6) . . . . . . ter
7) . . . . . . ter   8) . . . . . . ter   9) . . . . . . ter
10) . . . . . . ter   11) . . . . . . ter   12) . . . . . . ter

28. Find 12 words beginning and ending in G:

1) G . . . . . . g   2) G . . . . . . g   3) G . . . . . . g
4) G . . . . . . g   5) G . . . . . . g   6) G . . . . . . g
7) G . . . . . . g   8) G . . . . . . g   9) G . . . . . . g
10) G . . . . . . g   11) G . . . . . . g   12) G . . . . . . g

29. Find 12 eleven letter words.

1)   2)   3)
4)   5)   6)
7)   8)   9)
10)   11)   12)

30. Find 12 words beginning with SUB:

1) Sub......	2) Sub......	3) Sub......
4) Sub......	5) Sub......	6) Sub......
7) Sub......	8) Sub......	9) Sub......
10) Sub......	11) Sub......	12) Sub......

31. Find 12 words ending in LAR:

1) .....lar	2) .....lar	3) .....lar
4) .....lar	5) .....lar	6) .....lar
7) .....lar	8) .....lar	9) .....lar
10) .....lar	11) .....lar	12) .....lar

32. Find 12 words beginning with GRE:

1) Gre......	2) Gre......	3) Gre......
4) Gre......	5) Gre......	6) Gre......
7) Gre......	8) Gre......	9) Gre......
10) Gre......	11) Gre......	12) Gre......

33. Find 12 twelve letter words.

1)	2)	3)
4)	5)	6)
7)	8)	9)
10)	11)	12)

34. Find 12 words beginning with OB:

1) Ob.......	2) Ob.......	3) Ob.......
4) Ob.......	5) Ob.......	6) Ob.......
7) Ob.......	8) Ob.......	9) Ob.......
10) Ob.......	11) Ob.......	12) Ob.......

35. Find 12 words ending with BLE:

1) .....ble	2) .....ble	3) .....ble
4) .....ble	5) .....ble	6) .....ble
7) .....ble	8) .....ble	9) .....ble
10) .....ble	11) .....ble	12) .....ble

36. Find 12 words ending in NESS:

1) ......ness   2) ......ness   3) ......ness
4) ......ness   5) ......ness   6) ......ness
7) ......ness   8) ......ness   9) ......ness
10) ......ness   11) ......ness   12) ......ness

37. Find 12 two letter words.

1)   2)   3)
4)   5)   6)
7)   8)   9)
10)   11)   12)

38. Find 12 words beginning with DIS:

1) Dis......   2) Dis......   3) Dis......
4) Dis......   5) Dis......   6) Dis......
7) Dis......   8) Dis......   9) Dis......
10) Dis......   11) Dis......   12) Dis......

39. Find 12 words ending with OSE:

1) ......ose   2) ......ose   3) ......ose
4) ......ose   5) ......ose   6) ......ose
7) ......ose   8) ......ose   9) ......ose
10) ......ose   11) ......ose   12) ......ose

40. Find 12 words beginning with DEP:

1) Dep......   2) Dep......   3) Dep......
4) Dep......   5) Dep......   6) Dep......
7) Dep......   8) Dep......   9) Dep......
10) Dep......   11) Dep......   12) Dep......

Your Score

Each word is worth one point provided it exists. Your score equals the number of words you found.

Here are a few you might have found:

1. For example: *army, boat, curb, damp, easy, fare, gash, heal, inch, jury, keen, lane.*

2. For example: *probable, probate, problem, proceed, process, proclaim, prodigal, produce, profess, profile, profit, progress.*

3. For example: *bent, tent, sent, vent, went, parent, spent, potent, recent, repent, event, reverent.*

4. For example: *eagle, earache, ease, eclipse, edge, edible, eerie, elapse, elevate, eligible, elite, elsewhere.*

5. For example: *arrow, brash, cause, doing, ensue, field, grand, happy, irate, joint, kiosk, loyal.*

6. For example: *except, excerpt, exchange, excise, exclusive, excursion, exuse, execute, exempt, exert, exhale, exercise.*

7. For example: *gain, abstain, curtain, certain, bargain, fountain, villain, remain, refrain, detain, retain, maintain.*

8. For example: *tot, tut, tilt, tart, taut, tent, teat, toot, that, taint, tarot, ticket.*

9. For example: *aboard, bakery, camera, devote, escape, flaunt, gladly, happen, induce, jargon, kitten, length.*

10. For example: *image, imagine, imbecile, imitate, immaculate, immediate, immoral, immortal, immune, impact, impair, implore.*

11. For example: *direct, dissect, interject, bisect, connect, reject, perfect, protect, expect, inspect, respect, insect.*

12. For example: *label, loll, lull, lackadaisical, lateral, lawful, legal, lethal, level, libel, liberal, literal.*

13. For example: *aerobat, blemish, cascade, delight, egotist, flopped, gambler, holiday, initial, jubilee, knitted, liaison.*

14. For example: *transact, transcend, transcribe, transfer, transform, transgress, transit, translate, transmit, transparent, transpire, transpose.*

15. For example: *creature, picture, future, nature, torture, injure, figure, pleasure, measure, leisure, treasure, pressure.*

16. For example: *hash, high, hush, harsh, hatch, heath, hutch, hurrah, haunch, hunch, health, hyacinth.*

17. For example: *absentee, beginner, catapult, decadent, entrance, fiendish, gigantic, heirloom, interest, juvenile, knocking, lowering.*

18. For example: *comb, combat, combination, come, comedian, comfort, comic, command, comment, common, compass, compose.*

19. For example: *division, direction, fashion, passion, notion, promotion, station, ration, confusion, completion, companion, question.*

20. For example: *dabbed, damaged, danced, dated, dread, dead, divided, deceived, differed, directed, driven, dud.*

21. For example: *abolition, bristling, candidate, decorator, emergence, financial, geometric, haphazard, illegible, jellyfish, kidnapped, liquorice.*

22. For example: *preach, preamble, precarious, precaution, precede, precept, precinct, previous, precise, preclude, predominate, preface.*

23. For example: *sailor, tailor, protector, inspector, divisor, mirror, floor, anchor, superior, professor, visitor, doctor.*

24. For example: *noun, noon, nun, neon, nylon, napkin, nation, notion, neaten, neutron, newsmen, nocturn.*

25. For example: *achievable, blackberry, challenger, delightful, enthusiasm, felicitate, geographic, habitually, illiterate, juggernaut, kingfisher, legitimate.*

26. For example: *bias, bicker, bid, big, bile, brill, bind, biography, bisect, bit, bitchy, bizarre.*

27. For example: *duster, enter, cluster, fluster, muster, foster, better, stutter, preventer, banter, utter, letter.*

28. For example: *gag, gang, gaining, gaping, gasping, gazing, germinating, getting, giving, gloating, gracing, gripping.*

29. For example: *allegorical, benevolence, carefulness, deteriorate, ebulliently, fingerprint, grandmother, haberdasher, inattentive, justifiably, kindhearted, launderette.*

30. For example: *subconscious, subdue, subject, subjugate, sublime, submit, subscription, subside, substance, subterfuge, subtle, subtract.*

31. For example: *pedlar, pillar, caterpillar, scholar, collar, circular, regular, similar, cellar, stellar, annular, triangular.*

32. For example: *grease, great, greed, green, greet, gregarious, grey, grenadine, gremlin, grenade, grew, greyhound.*

33. For example: *accomplished, battleground, cancellation, desirability, encyclopaedia, featherbrain, gigantically, historically, indifference, jurisdiction, kaleidoscope, lighthearted.*

34. For example: *obedience, obelisk, obese, obey, object, obligation, oblige, oblique, obscene, obscure, obsess, obstacle.*

35. For example: *able, stable, miserable, table, vegetable, amiable, horrible, terrible, invisible, possible, impossible, incredible.*

36. For example: *business, sadness, harness, highness, smartness, gentleness, politeness, crudeness, righteousness, happiness, thoughtfulness, darkness.*

37. For example: *on, of, so, do, we as, is, an, at, to, if, by.*

38. For example: *disagree, disallow, disappear, disappoint, disarray, discerning, disciple, disclose, discourage, discreet, dish, disguise.*

39. For example: *hose, lose, those, impose, rose, whose, choose, propose, nose, suppose, cellulose, repose.*

40. For example: *depart, depend, depict, deplete, deploy, depose, depth, deputation, department, depress, deprice, deposit.*

How to Interpret Your Results

There were 480 words to find in all, which is roughly the number of words used in everyday speech.

Your score should normally be between 120 and 270 words. Above or below this, and your score is not really worth going by. Perhaps you didn't stick to the time limit (30 minutes), but whatever the case, this test is not for you.

- **Between 120 and 179 words 'found'**
  You are amongst the average. You have enough words at your disposal for everyday life and can express what you have to say even if you lack vocabulary occasionally.

- **Between 180 and 216 words 'found'**
  You have a good vocabulary level, can find words quickly and express yourself. You never lack the words to say what you want to, and have a certain degree of mental agility that allows you to adapt well to those you are being questioned by.

- **Between 216 and 270 words 'found'**
  You have an excellent vocabulary and are unbeatable at Scrabble. You use words with such ease as to be almost disconcerting. This doesn't necessarily make you a literary genius, but it is very practical in everyday life, if only to solve crosswords.

THE SPATIAL FACTOR

Thurstone's spatial (S) factor concerns intelligence in its primary ability to perceive shapes. The mechanics of intelligence presuppose this ability to make a precise representation of things.

Strictly speaking, it is an ability to perceive and analyse spatial configurations. But it also ties in with other factors and faculties such as the perception of three-dimensional configuration, visualisation, orientation and spatial memory.

Spatial orientation is the ability to recognise a structure regardless of the way it is presented.

Spatial memory, which is different from visual memory, concerns only the capacity to memorise spatial structures (geographical maps for example).

Visualisation is more concerned with the ability to make a mental picture of a three-dimensional movement.

Test your representation faculties

The following test, based on typical models, is made up of 20 illustrations. Each one represents a spatial configuration and presents a different problem. There is no strict time limit, but if you spend more than 30 minutes on it, it loses its efficacy.

I

Look at these bars for about 15 seconds. Then indicate which ones are the same length.

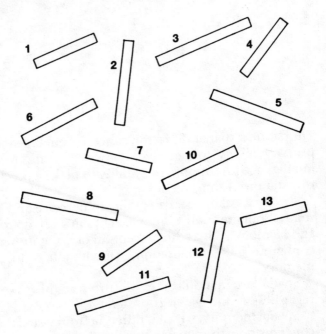

II

Look at these ties. How many different motifs are there?

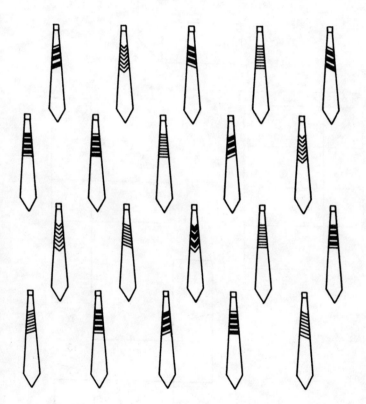

III

Look at this box. It is made by folding one of the three figures below it. Which one?

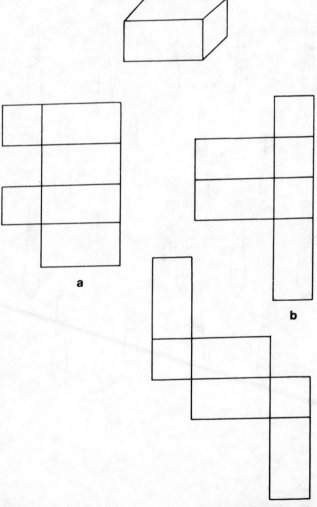

IV

Look at this figure. How many times are shapes a, b and c represented within it?

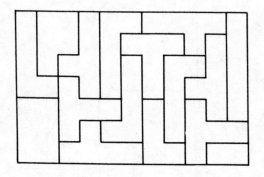

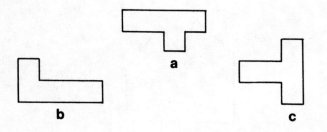

a

b

c

V

Look at this shape. With what other shape (a, b, c, d or e) does it form a rectangle?

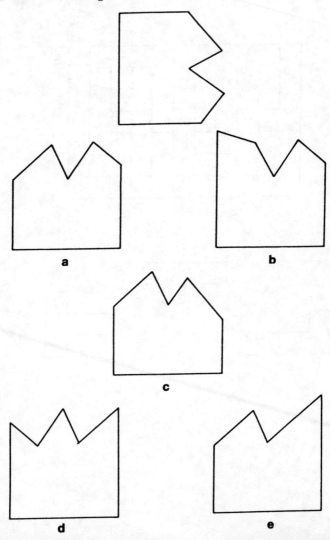

IV

Look at this figure. How many times are shapes a, b and c represented within it?

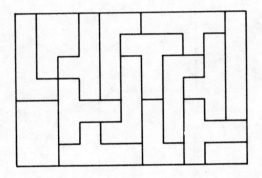

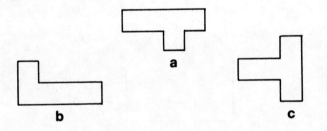

V

Look at this shape. With what other shape (a, b, c, d or e) does it form a rectangle?

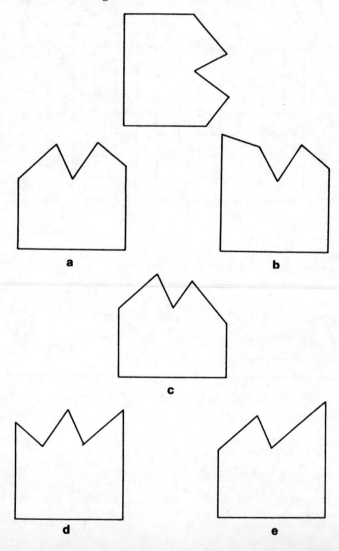

VI

Look at this picture carefully. How many chairs are there?

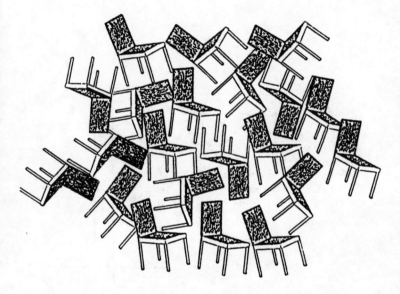

VII

Look at this shape. It has been made by folding one of the three figures below. Which one?

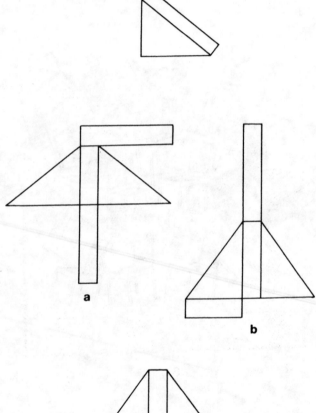

VIII

Look at this chessboard carefully for about 30 seconds. Take a mental note of the position of each piece. Now cover the board and find the position of the black knight from memory.

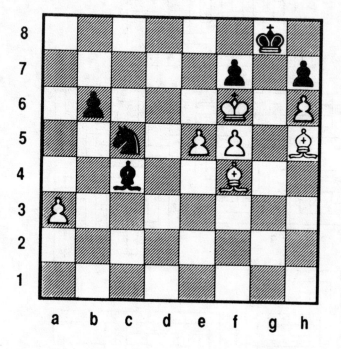

IX

Look at this mosaic. Which figure does it become (a, b, c or d) when it is turned 90° anticlockwise?

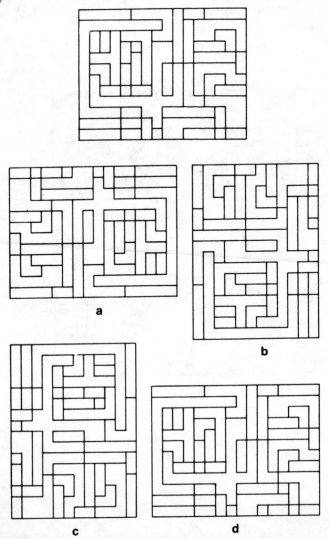

X

Look at this picture carefully. How many cats are there?

Plate XI

Look at the two shapes below. They're the same pyramid shown as a solid and flat. Put the shading shown on the solid onto the corresponding sides of the flat figure.

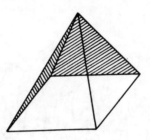

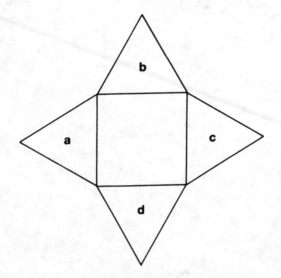

XII

Look at this shape. It has been made by folding one of the three figures below it. Which one?

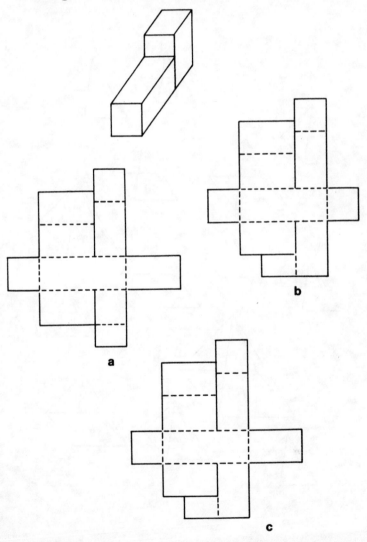

XIII

Look at these figures for about 15 seconds. Now indicate which ones are the same height.

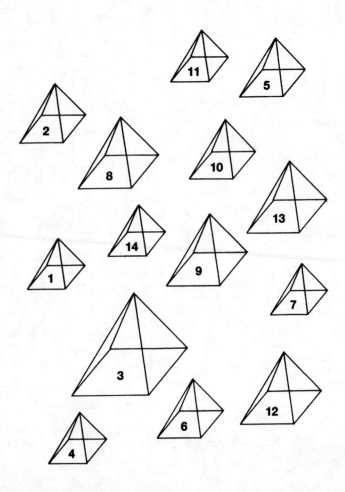

XIV

Look at this mosaic. How many times are shapes a, b, c, d and e represented within it?

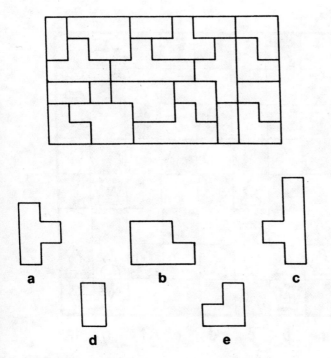

XV

Look at this chessboard for about 30 seconds. Take a mental note of the position of each piece. Now cover the board and find the position (number and letter) of the white king from memory.

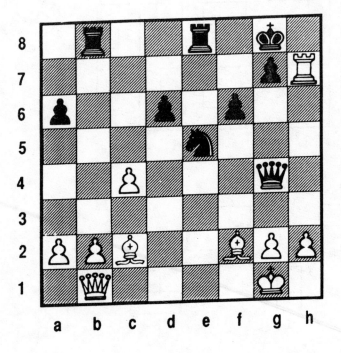

XVI

Look at the two shapes below. The same shape is represented once as a solid, and once flat. Put the black colouring shown on the solid onto the corresponding sides of the of the flat figure.

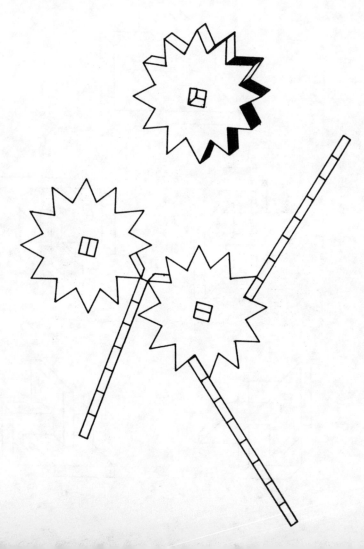

XVII

Look at this shape. Which figure (a, b, c or d) does it become when rotated 90° clockwise?

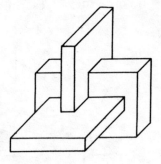

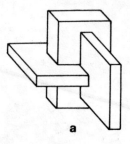

a

b

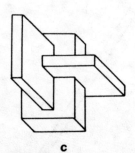

c

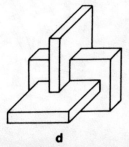

d

XVIII

Look at this shape. With which other shape does it become a box?

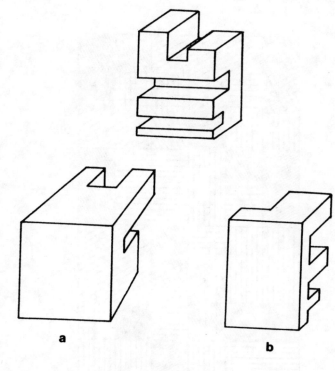

a

b

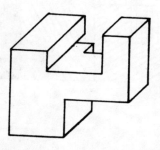

c

XIX

Look at this patchwork. How many different motifs are present?

XX

Look at this shape. It has been made by folding one of the three figures below (a, b or c). Which one?

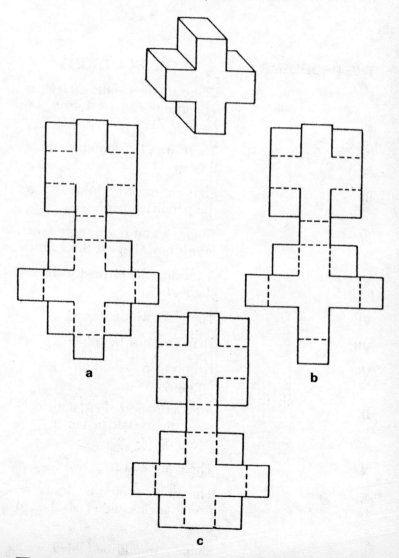

Your Score

Each correct answer is worth one point. Your score equals the number of correct answers you made in 30 minutes.

THE PROBLEMS	THE SOLUTIONS
I	There are three different lengths. The groups are: (1, 4, 7, 9, 13); (2, 6, 10, 12); (3, 5, 8, 11).
II	There are 11 different motifs on the ties.
III	Figure c must be folded to get the parallelepipede.
IV	Shapes a and b are represented four times. Shape c, three times.
V	A rectangle is formed with shape d.
VI	There are 21 chairs.
VII	Shape b must be folded.
VIII	Position C5 should be remembered.
IX	After a rotation of 90° anticlockwise, the mosaic becomes figure b.
X	There are 22 cats.
XI	The motifs should be drawn on two triangles: either ab, bc, cd or da.
XII	Shape c should be folded.

XIII   There are four different heights: (3); (8, 9, 12, 13); (2, 5, 6, 10) (1, 4, 7, 11, 14).

XIV   Shapes a and b are represented three times, shape c twice, shape d five times and shape e six times.

XV   Position G1 should be remembered.

XVI   The shape should be coloured like this:

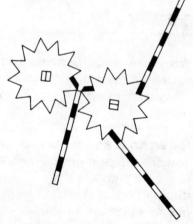

XVII   After a rotation of 90° clockwise, the shape becomes figure c.

XVIII   The shape becomes a box with figure b.

XIX   The patchwork is made up of seven different motifs (one black, 4 stripes and 2 crosses).

XX   Figure a should be folded to make the cross.

How to Interpret Your Results

You can interpret them in two ways; firstly as a whole, then by category.

Globally

The score is normally between 3 and 17 problems solved. Below or above this, and the test is no longer valid. Either that, or you are extremely dull or extremely gifted. This is very rare.

- **Between 3 and 9 correct answers:**
  You are amongst the average; upper average above 6, lower average less than 6. You are able to represent things in your mind fairly well, but the apparent complexity of certain problems sometimes prevents you from reasoning efficiently.

- **Between 10 and 13 correct answers:**
  As a whole, you have excellent representational faculties, but there are some problems you are presented with which throw you. You are sometimes a bit rigid in your way of thinking.

- **Between 14 and 17 correct answers:**
  You have astonishing representational faculties or are very lucky if you based too many of your answers on guess work. You often spatialise your problems in order to better solve them.

Category by Category

You can get a good idea of your weak and strong points.

- You have a good perception of spatial configurations if you scored best in problems: I, II, V, XIII, XVI, XVIII and XIX.

- On the other hand, you have an excellent sense of orientation if you scored best in problems: IV, VI, IX, X, XIV and XVII.

- Lastly, you have excellent visualisation if you scored best in problems: III, VII, XI, XII and XX.

- Problems VIII and XV (chessboards) are to do with spatial memory. Whether you got them right or wrong, the answers you gave are only of indicative value.

Opening doors to the World of books

Book Tokens

Book Tokens can be bought and exchanged at most bookshops